C000062279

Dear Ruth
A Lament for Africa

by Pamela Cotton

© Copyright 2009 Pamela Cotton.

All rights reserved. No part of this publication may be reproduced,
stored in a retrieval system, or transmitted, in any form or by
any means, electronic, mechanical, photocopying, recording, or
otherwise, without the written prior permission of the author.

First Published in 2009 by Milton Contact Ltd.

A CIP catalogue record for this book is available
from the British Library.

ISBN 978-0-9562649-0-9

Printed in UK

Milton Contact Limited
3 Hall End, Milton
Cambridge CB24 6AQ
United Kingdom
Order online at *www.miltoncontact.com*

Contents

Contents

Dedication

For Maximillian, Zachary, Benjamin, Thomas, Constance and any future family descendants on to the third and fourth generation.

Bygone Africa

Africa is part of me; it was love at first sight.

The sounds and smells of the African
Day, the noises of the night.

The slither of a snake in the grass, the
fluttering insects in the air, the little creatures
on the floor, pitter patter, pitter patter.

The hoot of an owl in a nearby tree, the
chameleon on the wall. 'you expats. are like
us', said he. 'You adapt, you soon adapt.'

The age-old villages, the deep throb of the drums
echoing through the bush with a message for
the villagers. Perhaps something is the matter.

The bustling cities, people at work, people
shopping for goods they cannot find, they
are not there. The thunder, the stillness, the
heat of the African noon, wrapped.

The tribal songs and dances full of life and meaning,
swirling and twirling under the setting sun.

Sitting round the cooking pot with their
maize porridge, rolling it into balls.

Relish in another dish, titbits of dried
fish, just enough to go round.

When darkness falls it is time to rest in their
little thatched huts, rondavals made of mud.

Curled up inside, a child cries, is soothed. They
fall asleep to the sound of animal calls.

Africa is part of me. It will for ever be with me,
Woven into my very soul for as long as I shall be.

One

The Beginning of my Personal African Experience

I was one of the last recruits to the Colonial Civil Service. In 1960 I applied to the Colonial Office for a post in the colonies, somewhere sunny and warm. After they had taken up a great many references, and I had completed their comprehensive application form, I was called for a two-day interview. I was asked whether I would be interested in Nyasaland. I said that would be lovely, without even knowing where Nyasaland was. By the time it came to the second interview I had done some homework and could speak more confidently about Nyasaland. All the interviewers were men, I noticed, and it was clear when they offered me a relatively high-powered job that I was going into a male-orientated world. I was appointed to the post of Social Development Officer in Nyasaland, in Central Africa, and after a period of preparation in London, and a medical examination at a classy clinic in Harley Street, I was sent out to take up the appointment. It was just a few years before the fall of the British Empire and the extinction of the Colonial Office.

I was young and ingenuous but full of enthusiasm for new happenings, and I loved it. During this period I wrote a number of letters to my friends back in UK telling them about life in Africa as I experienced it. These letters of course eventually ended up in the dustbins of the various recipients. All except those I sent to my friend Ruth. Ruth died in 2005, but there was a follow-up to her death. During 2007 I received a letter from her daughter Anne, enclosing a package addressed to me in Ruth's handwriting. When I opened the package I was astounded to find a pile of very old letters, tatty and torn, coffee stained and dirty, but nevertheless here they were, the very letters I had sent to Ruth from Africa during the 1960s and 70s. They covered my work experience, my marriage, the birth of our children, and descriptions of daily life in central Africa during the turbulence of the change from British rule to African rule. Ruth's last message to me was also in the package. It said "I kept your letters, to be returned to you one day, so that you may remember these years. They are a living history of a period in place and time, and your personal story will be of much interest to your great-great grandchildren and others of your descendants. I ask you to add any further comments you have to make, and write it all down especially for them."

The letters themselves could not be preserved. They had obviously been read and re-read, become raggedy, had things spilled on them. I had to hold some of them together to read them myself. But I transferred the relevant parts of them to my computer, and where they had jogged my memory of events, added a few facts. I do not think my descendants will find this history of a tiny period in time as interesting as Ruth imagined they would, but in memory of a dear friend whose loyalty and curious concern with my life always gave me a 'feel-good' boost, I have written it down. Old Grandpa Jim was immensely interested in history and read history books avidly until well into old age. Our youngest son Jeremy read History for his degree. Let us imagine that these notes may be of use in writing a history essay on the strange phenomenon of The British Empire, should one of the future members of our family be interested in it, and if students are still writing essays at the end of this century.

Two

Blantyre 1960

Dear Ruth,

At last I am in Blantyre. Getting here was a journey of discovery, and more stressful than I imagined it would be. I safely boarded the Caernarvon Castle mail ship at Southampton and shared an emotional farewell to England with the departing passengers, holding coloured streamers which went from the ship to the shore, and singing 'Wish me luck as You Wave me Good-bye', until the streamers broke and fell into the water as we set sail for a ten-day voyage to Cape Town, South Africa. I settled into a little cabin to which my cabin trunk had already been delivered, and then set off on an exploratory tour around the various decks. There was a library, a tiny swimming pool, a big area for deck games such as quoits and deck tennis, a large bar and lounge, a huge dining room, and all around decks full of sunbeds and small tables, to which an army of stewards would soon be delivering drinks and refreshments to the assortment of passengers, most of whom had extraordinarily large appetites. The dining room was a sight to behold. Gigantic meals were served there three times a day, but still people tended to leave with table napkins full of tit-bits in case they were hungry before the next batch of refreshments. Coffee, tea, and cake were available mid morning and mid afternoon. After so many years of frugal living I could not have imagined there are such greedy people in the world if I hadn't seen it with my own eyes. The voyage itself passed happily enough, reading books, playing games on deck, walking around the ship for exercise, chatting to my fellow passengers, and getting burned to blisters while sitting in the sun. We had to bath in

Pam

sea water and this was very painful when the blisters burst. The other passengers consisted of civil servants going back to their postings after home leave, missionaries doing the same, British settlers returning to their tea plantations and tobacco farms after taking rare holidays at home, and a few tourists going to visit relatives and explore parts of deepest Africa. They all seemed to know where they were going, and I felt very much the new recruit. We stopped off at Madeira on the way, and this was the highlight of the trip for me – getting on dry land again and seeing something new. Life at sea is not particularly inspiring. My greatest satisfaction was being paid a substantial salary for doing nothing. Eventually we arrived in Cape Town, and everybody gathered on deck to get a view of Table Mountain, over which the South Africans amongst us drooled. I was pleased the voyage had ended. I don't think I shall ever be attracted to a holiday on a cruise liner. Too much aimless loafing. and too much sea.

Getting from Cape Town to Blantyre was an adventure. I went to the station expecting that after a few hours train journey I would arrive at my destination. Not so. A friendly porter guided me to the right train and I found myself sharing a sleeper with a lady on her way to join her husband in Southern Rhodesia. She had a little girl with her. Fortunately she knew her way around and she informed me that I would take five days to get to Blantyre, and I would have to change at Bulawayo and at Salisbury on the way. The seats on the train could be changed into beds, and our meals were delivered to our compartment on trays. Washing facilities consisted of a small basin with a tap that dispensed cold water. This was 'First Class' travel, by the way. By the time we arrived in Bulawayo I was filthy with soot from the engine and insufficient washing. However, I was able to get a bath on Bulawayo station, and the journey to Salisbury only took one day. From Salisbury I took a train destined for Beira in Portuguese East Africa. These names and places were all new to me. On this train I had a sleeper to myself, but by taking a walk along the corridor I met fellow travellers one of whom told me I must get off the train at a place called Dondo junction and walk across the railway track to a railcar heading for Limbe, near Blantyre. He offered to show me the way since he was heading for the same place, and it was fortunate I met him, otherwise I might have gone all the way to Beira and become hopelessly lost. When we arrived at Dondo he duly escorted me across the track to the small waiting railcar. As we approached Nyasaland the weather became hotter and hotter and by the time we crossed the border at Port Herald it was absolutely stifling. My companion assured me that Blantyre was in the hills and therefore cooler. Needless to say, I revelled in the heat and felt sure I had come to the right place for me, though the mosquitoes were rather tiresome. I was glad I had been taking Panadol for the past ten days as a precaution against malaria. After some hours we pulled into Limbe station and I stepped on to the platform with some trepidation. All was well. A gentleman in tropical dress walked briskly towards me, hands outstretched "Miss McKee?" he asked, "Welcome to Nyasaland." This was Tommy Thompson, a senior civil servant involved in Social Development. Even more welcoming was the sight of the wooden crates I had packed in London many weeks before, carrying my few goods and chattels. There they were, being unloaded from the guards van of the railcar, and there also was the cabin trunk I had taken with me on the ship. My baggage had travelled with more confidence than I had. We climbed into a Land rover and travelled on the worst dirt road I had ever seen, bumping along over stones and pot holes to an outpost called Mpemba, where Tommy Thompson was based. He was in charge of a large training camp for African women and their children, a residential home for delinquent African youths, and the School of Public Administration for Africans training for jobs in the civil service, and this school, Tommy informed me, was where I would give my lectures.

What lectures, I wonder? There were various out-buildings for an assortment of classes in household management, sewing, cooking skills and such like, and there was a staff of British nurses and teachers and some elderly white women who had been born in Nyasaland to an early settler and had useful local knowledge. There were various others whose specific jobs I could not identify. Here I was to spend my first few days in Nyasaland. I stayed with Tommy Thompson and his wife, who were both very kind. The wife set about teaching me to behave as a British woman in Africa should, and she found for me a servant she called 'the boy'. His name is Willard. I think one of the Arab traders must have played a part in his birth because he has an Arabic look about him, and he is Muslim.

Very soon I moved on to begin my life in Blantyre, but my days at Mpemba were most useful. I was given a quick orientation course, including visits to rural African villages in the Blantyre region. There were no surprises here. They are exactly as geography teachers had described long ago when I was at school. The people live in mud huts with thatched roofs, and are very inter-dependent, rather like a huge extended family. Water has to be fetched and carried in buckets from some source away from the settlement. They cook outside on open fires, or sometimes in the rainy season, on the floor inside the house. Their staple diet is mealy meal porridge made from maize, with a 'relish' of dried fish or, occasionally, a little meat. People from the villages who work in town return home regularly with goodies from the shops, or send back money with which things can be bought. There is a Village Headman, and a 'Chief', who exercise considerable power over their people. Well, this is how it seems to me on first viewing. I am told there can be a problem with the children's diet because the men get the best pickings from any food that is available, then the women, and the children come a poor third. I did not look at the local sanitation because I instinctively knew it would be disagreeable.

After this I was taken to Soche, an African township near Blantyre for Government employees who work in the town. Their families live here too. There is a community centre housing a library, rooms for social functions, meeting rooms, and other facilities. This, I was told, is where my African staff live.

Also during these first days I was shown my office in the Government Building and introduced to some of the staff. I also met my boss, Sydney, who has the office next door. He is the 'Officer in Charge of Social Development for Nyasaland' and he should be in the capitol, Zomba, with all the other Departmental Heads, but he asked for a base in Blantyre to be near his lady friend Francis. She is a nurse, and works for the British Red Cross. I have been told that Sydney has a wife and two children in England.

While I was inspecting my office with its desk, filing cabinets, chairs, and a safe for keeping the Public Assistance vote, the Information Officer, a chap called John, came to interview me so that he could write something about me in the local paper. Tall and important-looking, with pen poised over a note book, he wrote down a few sentences. He told me he had just moved into a new house in Kanjedza, and I was going to be one of his neighbours. I don't know whether that's good news or bad.

That's all for now. I am going to Zomba for Christmas to stay with the family of the person who rescued me on the train and put me on the railcar at Dondo. He has four children so it will not be restful, but it will be interesting to see what happens in the capitol city, as it is called. It is said to be even smaller than Blantyre, and Blantyre is small. I will write again in the New Year. Since Christmas is two months away I shall know by then much more about colonial life, and working in Africa, and whether I am going to love it or hate it.

Blantyre 1961–1962

Dear Ruth,

I love it here. As you can imagine, the climate is so very much more hospitable than it is in Britain and I never cease to gloat over it. Blantyre is 3,000 feet above sea level which means it is never unbearably hot. Summer temperatures are consistently in the 80s and 90s F, and even in winter it only gets on the cold side at night and in the early mornings. Knowing me, you will appreciate what a blessing this is. Household heating is not necessary, although it is surprising how cold even 70% can feel when the temperature sinks to this level. Sometimes I have to go on a sort of safari to much hotter places, and I like that too. The one thing I don't like is the high rainfall in the wet season. It comes in the form of tropical storms so violent that everything stops while the rain is falling, the thunder roaring and the lightening warring. The storms don't last for long but they leave such a mess. The dirt roads become muddy and water-logged and they are almost impassable until the sun dries them up, and outside the town most roads are of this type. I have to make frequent visits to Mpemba. The road to it is diabolical and sometimes my car gets bogged down in mud, and I am stuck. Amazingly, the once empty road is quickly full of activity as a cluster of laughing Africans seem to appear from nowhere and they push me out.

I have a very nice bungalow-type house all to myself, complete with government telephone. It is like living in luxury after my minute London flat. It is in a place called Kanjedza a mile or so outside Blantyre, a place entirely full of government housing for British civil servants, apart from a few members of the Kings African Rifles, that is, the army. Most of the houses would not look out of place in an affluent suburb of London, complete with pretty flower gardens, well-watered lawns, and vegetable patches. It is all very pleasant. However, it took me some time to get to grips with the domestic side of life. Moving into my house was a nightmare. It is brand new, and when I arrived builders' mess was everywhere, amongst the government furniture which was already in situ. I was delivered here, together with my baggage, and with my boy, Willard, and dumped on the doorstep. Willard is the most valuable asset I have acquired in this country. He looked firmly at my helpless state and said, 'Donna, I clean up. You go and meet the neighbours.' The neighbours were all agog and very ready to be met. I went next door and chatted to the lady there, while keeping half an eye on the house. Willard had put together a group of other peoples' servants and they were all beavering away with brooms and mops and buckets of water and trash cans. Several hours passed before I went back, by which time the place had been transformed into something that seemed orderly, and Willard was ready to tell me how much I lacked in terms of equipment. My crates had been opened and peered into and he was writing a list of things that must be bought, and they included vast amounts of utensils he would need for cooking, a full dinner service for eight people, napkins, table cloths, masses of different types of glasses and many other items too numerous to mention. Even vases for flowers were on the list, and I've never found much use for those. It made the few cups and plates and cutlery etc. I had brought from England look hugely inadequate.

'But why do I need so much?' I asked. 'There is only me.'

'Entertaining Donna' he said firmly'. More of that anon.

Fortunately, for the first time in my life I am not short of money, and later I took Willard's list and bought the lot. That first evening the press officer John arrived to see how I was getting on. He looked into my empty cupboards and said the most immediate thing to do was to get in supplies, particularly supplies of alcoholic beverages. He agreed to collect me after getting home from work the following day and take me to the European Supermarket to put things right.

Another hardship to begin with was the fact that my car, a brand new Ford Anglia I had shipped out from England, was still somewhere on the high seas. A driver was sent to pick me up for the office, but it was not the same as having one's own transport. At lunch time on my first day at work I was told I should come to The European Club. Not having much choice, I went, and found myself standing round a bar with a group of jolly people.

'What will you have to drink?' asked a woman called Marjory. My request for an orange juice was met with disbelieving amusement.

'Well, I don't usually drink at lunch time', I protested.

'You do now' said Marjory forcefully, and ordered two gins and tonic.

Marjory is a middle-aged stenographer used to getting her own way. Stenographers are called secretaries in England. I tasted my gin and tonic and found it very much to my liking. We both had another one, and thus began my love affair with the gin bottle. Office hours are from 7.00 a.m until 12.00 p.m., and then from 3.00 p.m. until around 6.00 p.m., and so, on mornings spent in the office, there is plenty of time to take a lunch break.

When all the above-mentioned teething troubles were over I settled down happily. I must say I very much approve of this servant system. I now have two boys. Willard insisted that this is necessary, and, as it turns out, he is absolutely right. Thus I have John, a young lad who does the garden, chops wood for the wood stove water heater outside, and cleans the car. My lovely Willard, probable age around thirty, does the cooking, washing and housework. Everything is accomplished with no more than a little supervision on my part, and I do not have to bother too much about things domestic. Nowadays I too have a pretty bungalow with colourful flowers, a well-watered lawn, and a vegetable patch. I know you won't believe that, but it is true. I fear I shall be less domesticated than ever by the time I return to England. I feel very guilty about how little the servants are paid: £4.50 a month for Willard and £3.00 for John + a few shillings a week posho for food, but I am assured this is the going-rate and it would be unwise to step out of line. I also buy their uniforms, and they live in a little house at the bottom of the garden where they have a maize patch for their mealy meal. Willard is Muslim, as I have told you, and John is Christian, the product of a mission school. They are both literate in both Chinyanja and English. Chinyanja is one of the local African languages, and I am supposed to learn it. The boys visit their respective villages once a week. Willard has Friday off and John has Sunday, and I think Willard had this in mind when he brought John along and asked me to give him a job. It means I have no servantless days, though I have to try hard not to entertain on a Friday. If Willard lived in England he could easily be employed as a chef, whereas John's cooking skills are as basic as my own.

Willard was not joking when he talked about entertaining. It is one of my duties. I am called upon to provide dinners and conversation for various dignitaries that come out from UK on tours of inspection, including people from the United Nations, occasional politicians, and leaders of charities that are represented out here, such as the Save the Children Fund and the Red Cross, It sounded daunting when I first knew about it, but in fact it is fun. Willard decides on the menu (always good), cooks the food, and cheerfully acts as waiter. I provide the conversation by inviting stimulating others, including men who know how to serve the drinks. Willard was also right about that dinner service for eight.

To make up for the blissful domestic state of affairs, work here is even more demanding than it is at home. Sometimes I feel quite overwhelmed with responsibility, and it is important not to take it all too seriously. I am in charge of Social Development in the Southern Province. The area stretches from Fort Johnson near the southern end of Lake Nyasa to Port Herald in the far south near to the border post. If you look at a map of Nyasaland you'll see it is a large area. I have a counterpart in the Northern Province called Liz Jevons, and a man in the Central Province whose name I forget. I have to control seven African Assistants all of whom are designated Probation Officers, as indeed am I. Although I know what Probation Officers do I have never before been responsible for anybody on probation. I also have the relevant number of clerks, messengers and so forth working in various offices, and two drivers for travelling in the bundu where a Land Rover is needed. But I am used to working with people and can manage the staff very well. It is the administration that bothers me most. I have control of quite a large amount of money and have to allocate resources appropriately, and write a monthly report on how the money has been spent. Not to worry. This whole country is full of small people trying to do big jobs, and somehow things run relatively smoothly.

The work itself is very varied. We have to cope with every type of problem, and amongst all races – African, Asian, Coloured, and European. We deal with destitutes, repatriates, children and young people, physically handicapped, mental defectives, matrimonial cases, probation, school welfare, after care cases, blind people, mentally sick, approved school and prison discharges, deportees from South Africa. And so it goes on in a never-ending stream. As funds are limited and facilities for helping such people practically nil you can imagine we don't get very far towards rehabilitation, at least not by British standards. We just soldier on, pleading for help from voluntary individuals and bodies such as the Red Cross and the Young Muslim Brotherhood. At least life is never dull. Myself, I do all the work that comes along in the European community. Most of the rest I delegate to my staff and in difficult cases they just come to me for a final decision on what is to be done about the problem.

Political life out here is a perpetual musical comedy. Dr Hastings Banda is the leader of the Malawi Congress Party. He drives around in a big black car, surrounded 'fore and aft by lines of Land Rovers and dispatch riders, and everything stops as he sails by, and he expects all to bow before him. There is a certain amount of tension below the surface, and sometimes one wonders where it is all going to end. But it is fascinating to watch developments. Our Department has just changed its Minister. It is now under Mr Chiume, a nasty little man who thinks he is the cat's whiskers. At the moment he is in London with Dr Banda so we are getting a bit of peace. He is a real dictator and no doubt we shall all get our instructions when he returns. I only hope that during his recent travels he has acquired some information about social welfare, otherwise he might well close down the Department and concentrate on football matches and things that will make a big splash, since that is the general trend.

Luckily I have no political trouble with my staff. They are all intelligent enough to know Dr Banda is not God. But sometimes it becomes an issue in one's work amongst the Africans. I have just completed a survey of the handicapped in Chief Chitera's area, near Zomba, an area containing 10,000 people. It took weeks to get it going. The Chief and his councillors co-operated well enough right from the start. But a body known as The Malawi League of Youth objected because there was no gen about the survey at their Party Headquarters. They went round telling all the village headmen that we were stooges for the United Federal Party, and that we were going to dig a big hole, put all their handicapped people into it, and bewitch them. This of course resulted in such people being sent off to hide in the bush. In the end I managed to get a letter from Chiume giving the survey his blessing, and consequently the blessing of the Malawi Party. We were then able to proceed. I used the students I was training at the School of Public Administration in Mpemba as interviewers, and called it "Practical Work" When Chiume became our Minister he closed this school for some reason best known to himself, but I had finished most of the lectures I intended to give by then. Sydney and I have been training African social workers for the future; he does the Law and Administration lectures, and I do Social Work Practice in its various forms, and Interviewing Techniques.

Social life out here is hectic. I go through phases when one of the biggest problems is what to wear to go to what with whom. I am a member of various clubs, including the Limbe Country Club, the Mlanje Mountain Club, and the Nyasaland Flying Club. The Flying Club is really only a glorified social club with the somewhat doubtful advantage of having a fleet of minute aeroplanes in which one can jolt around over Nyasaland. But it is about forty miles from Blantyre and makes a pleasant run out in the car. We are now in the middle of the tennis season and that keeps me busy most week-ends. I have rather rashly entered for the Limbe Championships in the Mixed Doubles and the Ladies Singles. Oh well, it will only involve two matches after all.

A month or so ago I went with a friend called Jim to spend a week-end at Monkey Bay on the shores of Lake Nyasa. The Lake is about 160 miles from here on poor roads so it was quite a long journey for a week-end, but it was heavenly, very hot, and calm and peaceful. We spent the time swimming and sun-bathing and messing about in boats. On the Sunday morning we asked an African to row us out to a little island completely uninhabited by human beings. The only signs of life were tropical fish, brightly coloured birds, and a few snakes. There were no paths so we were not able to explore it very thoroughly, but we went round it in the boat, stopping at various points en route. It was glorious to be absolutely free from work and politics and private engagements, and all the things that crowd one's life in Blantyre. While we were in Monkey Bay we also rowed out to the look-alike 'Chauncey Maples', the ship in which Dr Livingstone and the early missionaries did their work. We were able to get on board, and it was fascinating.

We are allowed twelve days a year local leave and I am due to take mine, and so is Jim. He has offered to take me to have a look round the Rhodesias and I am looking forward to that. We are hoping to cram quite a lot into it.

That is the end of my ramblings for 1962.

Blantyre 1963

Dear Ruth,

They say that time speeds by more rapidly as you get older so Heaven knows what it will be like in twenty years from now. I don't know where to begin with all my news because a lot has happened in the past few months. Maybe I should begin by telling you about Jim, since we are now married! He is a telecommunications engineer, aged 30, comes from London, though grew up in Wales as a war time evacuee. His full name is James Frederick Cotton, and he has been in Nyasaland for eight years. I find being called Mrs Cotton very strange. I preferred my own name, McKee, and it seemed a pity to have to give it up, but there it is. Jim works for the Federal Government (of Rhodesia and Nyasaland) and, as you probably know, the Federation has been disbanded. Therefore things are very unsettled at the moment and we don't know what the future may hold. We are just living a day at a time and hoping for the best.

To go back a little in time, we had a wonderful holiday in the Rhodesias last year, and it was during this holiday that we became engaged. Jim knew his way around and what to expect, but for me it was all new and exciting. Crossing the border into Southern Rhodesia was an inspiration. Suddenly the roads were well-maintained and good, the bridges were properly constructed, and there was an atmosphere of orderliness and regulation even in the rural areas. When we arrived in Salisbury I was dumbfounded. Here was a wonderful town that could compete with most British cities. It was great to see the bright lights, the people, the traffic, the shops, the parks, and the general purposeful bustle. It was so amazingly different from the Africa I had seen up until then, and I was indeed amazed. The people have a sense of 'belonging' to the place. Now I understand why the federal civil servants who were posted from Rhodesia to Nyasaland seem permanently homesick, and regard Nyasaland as a punishment station. From Salisbury we went on to Bulawayo, another wonderful, well-run town that I liked even more because it is warmer, and the people more friendly. We visited friends of Jim in both towns, and in these people I noticed the same sense of permanence, of being at home. This is quite different from being part of the colonial civil service, where one is never sure what will happen next, or where one might be tomorrow.

Our next port of call was the Wankie Game Reserve, and this was fun. We stayed in a well-appointed rondavel, and an African cooked meals for us on an outside fire. We went on tours of exploration and we viewed most type of game, including lion, elephant, rhino, giraffe, wart hog, all kinds of buck, and much more. Jim had seen it all before, but for me it was thrilling. After that we went on to the Victoria Falls and Livingstone, on the border with Northern Rhodesia. The Falls are truly magnificent. The Africans call them Musi-oa-Tunya: The Smoke that Thunders. Our last interesting stop in Rhodesia was at Kariba to see the famous Kariba Dam.

This is a tremendous engineering project, although, as predicted, many workers lost their lives during the building of it, and there is a monument beside the dam in memory of those who died. The dam doubles up as a leisure resort, used a lot for sailing and fishing. The friends we stayed with have a motor boat and one of their pleasures is to go out and tow in the sail boats when the wind drops, as it frequently does. After all that it was time to start the journey north, back to Nyasaland. We travelled through Northern Rhodesia via Lusaka, crossing the border near Fort Jamieson. Our last week-end was spent at Salima, beside Lake Nyasa, recovering from our travels. We covered over 3,000 miles in a fortnight.

Back in Blantyre Banda had returned from a Conference in London delighted with the outcome and the general turn of events. Political life seems less comical now that he and his merry men are getting their way all along the line. We have a stern dictatorship here. Anybody who dares to express criticism of the new 'Malawi', as Nyasaland will soon be called, is out on his neck forthwith. Several British civil servants have already "resigned" because of this, and one poor fellow who had named his dog Banda some time ago was deported with the others. One merely has to say the wrong thing in the wrong place and deportation follows. Morale amongst my colleagues is very low. The 'permanent and pensionable' types who have worked for the Colonial Office for many years are desperately hanging on to their jobs by grovelling to the African Ministers in the most nauseating way possible. Most of them are waiting hopefully for Independence Day, and the "lumpers" they think is due to them for services rendered. I hope they won't be disappointed. The British Government at times is somewhat unreliable in these matters. It is different for me, and others who were more recently appointed. We are here on contract, and had no intention of staying here for the rest of our lives, though I now know what a wonderful life I could have had if Macmillan's 'wind of change' had not blown across Africa.

I am soldiering on with my job in the same way as before. I have not been meddled with very much, and I am lucky enough to have reasonable staff who happily accept my leadership. They are in fact quite worried about what is happening in the country. I am indeed fortunate because some officers have suffered a good deal from insubordination on the part of their African staff since the London Conference. After all, it is their country now.

Thus, the Federation of Rhodesia and Nyasaland is dead, and The Malawi Youth held a big procession for its burial. For five hours on a Saturday morning a big black mass of humanity paraded through the streets of Blantyre carrying banners and slogans. They had made an enormous coffin which was held aloft, and was buried in the grounds of Banda's Blantyre residence, now known as the Presidential Palace. You can imagine what chaos it caused. The movement of traffic was completely stopped on a busy Saturday morning at the end of the month, when people came from far and wide to get their monthly food supplies from what are virtually the only shops in Nyasaland.

There is a good deal of intimidation of the mass of Africans, that is the people in the villages who are still very primitive. If they do not become members of the Malawi Party they are in danger of having their houses burned to the ground, often with them inside. One cannot help feeling that Britain has deserted them. Certainly this is an African country and will eventually be governed by Africans. But British politicians tend to forget that the Africans seen round a conference table in London belong to the educated minority, very much a minority I may say. By educated I mean educated overseas in places such as London. Dr Banda, for instance, is a medical doctor who worked for some time in the East End of London before coming back to Nyasaland to save his people from their colonial masters. There are many schools for African children here in the towns, run by the British, and the children who go to them get ten years or so basic schooling. But outside the towns, where the rest of the African population live in tribal villages, there are only services provided by the missionaries, and the vast majority do not live near enough to a Mission Station to take advantage of them. Thus the average African in Malawi still has a long way to go. Even most of my staff, who are amongst the most educated people in the country, still eat with their fingers sitting on the floor round a cooking pot. So at that Conference Table in London the Africans that we who are here live amongst and work amongst had no voice.

Let's get away from work and the inevitable politics. The big event of the year for Jim and me was our wedding on 23rd March. We were married very quietly in Blantyre in the office of the Registrar General. There were just four witnesses, Sydney and Francis for me, and friends of Jim, Tom and Eunice, for him. But that evening we had a big party at Ryalls Hotel, the local venue for many celebrations and stylish functions. Most of our colleagues and friends were there, and a good time was had by all. Too good for some people. We ended the night by taking friends back home with us because they were legless, and totally unable to drive back to Zomba. One of them was sick all night. Until this time Jim had his own house, also in Kanjedza, but he had just moved into mine because it is the most comfortable, and I have the best servants. For our honeymoon we took our local leave and went by plane to Durban in South Africa, where we had a great time exploring the Natal coast. Then it was back to life in Blantyre.

At the last AGM of the tennis section at Limbe Club Jim was elected Chairman and I was elected Secretary. This happened only recently, and is rather intimidating because we are by no means amongst the best tennis players in the country. It means

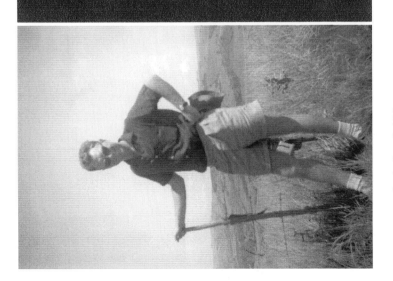

Pam and Jim wedding portrait

*Jim in South Africa,
shortly after we were married*

we have to organise the usual Saturday social tennis and be involved with teams for the league. The captains of both the A and B teams are on the committee so very likely all will be well.

With Independence for Malawi on its way, nobody knows how long any of us will remain in Nyasaland but we are making the most of it while we are here. A short time ago we spent a week-end in Fort Johnson on the southern tip of the Lake. It was tremendously hot, and seemed to have the biggest mosquitoes in Nyasaland. We stayed with a disreputable Irish bachelor who doesn't even believe in the refinement of mosquito nets, and we were glad to get back to Blantyre at the end of it. Fort Johnson is now something of a ghost town, but it is a fascinating place. In the early days it was the biggest centre of European population in the country due to the fact that it could be approached by river from other parts of Africa. It is full of the graves of the early missionaries, most of whom died from malaria. There is a very old Club there, and in it are many interesting records. For example, with reference to Mount Mlanje there is a recommendation that one uses a Mountain Machilla for climbing the mountain. There is a picture of a Mountain Machila in the record book. It appears to have been a long stout pole in the middle of which was a canvas seat with two holes in it for the legs of the climber. The pole was yoked to two sturdy Africans, one at each end, and the European braving the climb sat in the seat with a leg in each hole. Then off they went, with the Africans bearing most of the weight while the chap in the middle bent forward and moved his legs in walking mode.

"This", says the record, "relieves the strain on the legs no end"!

Nowadays we climb Mlanje in the conventional way, and admittedly it is a very steep climb.

Also in the records are somewhat moth-eaten letters from the first Governor of the country giving advice about the wellbeing of Europeans. One such letter says that:

"The health and welfare of the Europeans must always be the first consideration, and nothing will be too much to spend on achieving this."

How times have changed.

Some Facts About Malawi

Malawi, or Nyasaland, as it was called by the British, was where I began my life in Africa.

Malawi is a landlocked country in central Africa, bordered by Zambia, Tanzania and Mozambique. It was the poorest and least developed of the southern central African states, and it still is one of the poorest and least-developed countries in the world. It lacks natural resources and is densely populated by a mostly rural population; one of its chief exports is migrant labour to South Africa, where it is easier to make a living.

Just a small number of hunter-gatherers inhabited the area now known as Malawi until it was settled in the 10th century by various African Bantu tribes each with its own system of rule, with a tribal Chief and Village Headman. They built their villages on a chosen bit of territory and lived by subsistence farming. Soon after 1600 native tribesmen began trading with the Portuguese traders as one people, but by 1700 they had reverted to control by many individual tribes and this system of native rule lasted until the land was colonised by the British in1891.

In 1859 the Scottish missionary, explorer, and adventurer, David Livingstone, reached the shores of the long narrow lake that is a dominant feature of this country, bringing Christianity and the beginning of western civilisation to the region. At the time most of the indigenous people spoke a language called Chinyanja, and in that language the word for lake is Nyasa, and so the English called it Lake Nyasa. Livingstone was soon followed by other missionaries, and by traders, hunters and farmers, mostly from Britain.

In 1891 Britain established it as a British Protectorate and colonial civil servants were sent there to manage its affairs. They began to develop it in the British way of things. In 1907 it was named Nyasaland. The country jogged along without too many problems until 1953, when the territory was joined with Northern and Southern Rhodesia to form the Federation of Rhodesia and Nyasaland, despite strong objections by the African population. The administration of affairs was shared between British civil servants and federal civil servants.

To some federal civil servants posted to this region and charged with the management of Nyasaland it was regarded as a punishment station because it was so undeveloped and lacking in modern comforts. Others enjoyed the challenge of a safari-type lifestyle, and relished the testing conditions. By the time I arrived there the main towns had been developed and most services were up and running.

The unpopular Federation was dissolved on 31st December 1963, and, as part of the great retreat from Empire, Britain granted Nyasaland independence in 1964 under the name of Malawi. Independence Day was 6th July, and the first President was Dr Hastings Banda, who, it was claimed, lived to be 101 years old.

After independence in 1964 the territory became a one-party state. The first president, Hastings Banda, remained in charge until1994 and held full sway over the country until he was ousted from power in 1994. During his presidency Banda held the country together, but the economy declined and the people became poorer.

Malawi is now a democratic republic, multi-party state. It is pro-Western and has established a pro-Western foreign policy, which has insured many donors to Malawi, including a lot of help from the United States.

Malawi has good relations with most countries. The country maintained good relations with South Africa throughout the apartheid period which strained relations with other African states but nowadays strong diplomatic relationships are maintained with all other African countries.

The government faces challenges in the economy at the moment and it depends heavily on outside aid. Refugees from Rwanda and other African states often end up in Malawi and this draws aid in significant amounts. The country is riddled with AIDS. which puts a strain on government expenditure.

The superstar Madonna founded an organisation called Raising Malawi to help AIDS orphans in Malawi. It built an orphan care centre, and Madonna paid for a documentary about the hardships of Malawian orphans. Raising Malawi also works with a project called the Malawian Villages Project to improve health care, education and agriculture in the country.

Tribal conflict, once customary, has diminished somewhat and there appears to be the beginning of the concept of Malawian nationality. The population is mainly made up of native peoples, but Malawi did not throw the baby out with the bath water after independence and there are also Asians and European settlers living there. Several languages are spoken and there are numerous religious beliefs. English is the official language. Malawian culture combines native and colonial aspects, including music and dance, sport, art and crafts, wood carving and basket making.

The main agricultural products of Malawi include potatoes, corn, cattle and goats. Tobacco, tea and sugarcane are also still exported. But Malawi has always been a poor country, and it still is. It is estimated that more than half of the African population live below the poverty line.

Malawi 2008

When we were in South Africa early this year we wandered along the coast at Port Elizabeth and came across a large collection of home made African goods aimed at the tourists. We stopped to look, and there we met a Malawian called Chris. My husband Jim spoke to him in Chinyanja, one of the native languages of Malawi, and he was absolutely delighted. He gave us one of his pictures in memory of our days in Malawi long ago, and we bought several other products from him. He spoke of the sufferings of his people because of poverty and lack of services. He comes from a village near Lilongwe. He is an illegal immigrant to South Africa and is frequently escorted by the police back across the border, but he knows his way around the bush and is soon back again. He is there to earn money to support his family back in his home village. The picture he gave us is an impressionistic painting of African women dancing a tribal dance. He has never seen the inside of an art shop and the picture is painted with ordinary household paints. We framed it and put it behind glass, and it is now hanging in the hall of our flat. We shall treasure it.

Three

Some Facts About Zimbabwe

"Blessed be the land of Zimbabwe". That is the first line of the Zimbabwean National Anthem, and it was indeed a blessed land. Zimbabwe inherited the most well-developed, economically sound country in the whole of Africa. The new country had everything going for it. This was recently proclaimed anew by Archbishop Desmond Tutu, the South African clergyman and a tireless opponent of racial segregation, winner of the 1984 Nobel Peace Prize. The Archbishop roundly condemned Robert Mugabe and his cronies for the catastrophic state of the country and the humanitarian crisis created by them and he called for international action to stop the rot "Mugabe must be removed from power", said he. He seems to have been unheard. The suffering of the Zimbabwean people continues, and now the situation has been made even worse by an outbreak of cholera, with dying Zimbabweans crawling across the border into South Africa to find help. With no sanitation and no water the outcome was predictable.

98% of the population of Zimbabwe is made up of black ethnic groups. Official languages are Shona, Ndebele, and English. The majority people are Shona, about 84%. The second largest group, the Ndelebe, account for around 15%. Then there are Bantus from other ethic groups, and a few Asians. Also there are still a very tiny number of white Zimbabweans, mostly of British origin, still living in the country. During 2007 the economic situation and repressive political actions led to a quarter of the population fleeing to other countries, mainly to South Africa.

There was a Bantu civilisation in the Zimbabwe region early in the Middle Ages which seems to have been Shona. The evidence is the ruins of Great Zimbabwe. This city was built using an amazing dry stone architecture which appears to be unique. There are smaller ruins on smaller sites built in the same way. In the tenth century trade was taking place with the Phoenicians on the Indian Ocean coast which led to development during the eleventh century. The country traded gold, ivory and copper in return for glass and cloth. But Portuguese settlers destroyed the trade in a series of wars that by the early seventeenth century left the territory in a state of collapse. In 1834 the Ndelebe people came to Zimbabwe, making a new home for themselves called Matabeleland.

The Colonial history of Zimbabwe began in the same way as in the other two southern central African states. It was explored in the nineteenth century by European missionaries, notably David Livingstone. But it was founded as a result of the activities of Cecil Rhodes, a successful British businessman, and a man of great wealth and influence. He worked in South Africa but was thinking, as he often did, about increasing the spread of the British Empire in Africa. In 1888 he went to London and persuaded the British Prime Minister, Lord Salisbury, to grant a royal charter whereby he and his associates were entrusted with the occupation, control, and development of this part of Africa. It led in 1889 to the formation of the British South Africa Company aimed at colonising the area and encouraging trade and commerce. A pioneer column of settlers and police set off on a trek from Bechuanaland (now Botswana), and in September 1890 reached the site of Rhodesia's future capital. They called their camp Fort Salisbury. At first the land controlled by the British South Africa Company was called Zambesia, but in 1895 it was officially named Rhodesia in honour of Cecil Rhodes. Through a combination of expertise, money, determination, doggedness and sheer hard work the settlers prospered. They brought their western civilisation and culture with them and they turned Southern Rhodesia, later known simply as Rhodesia, into a land fit for the gods. Their cities of Salisbury, Bulawayo, and Umtali could compare favourably with many cities in Europe.

After World War One the British settlers began to ask for self-government. In 1923 they were given internal self-government and were taken over as a British Colony. The colony prospered, with the development of agriculture, and cattle-raising added to the original gold mining. Godfrey Huggins became Prime Minister in 1933. He wished to build a country based on Cecil Rhodes' ideal of "equal rights for all civilised men". Merit not skin colour would be the test of advancement; and political power would not be entrusted to the Africans until they became experienced enough to know how to use it.

Then, in 1953, the Federation of Rhodesia and Nyasaland was formed. On the whole the white settlers supported this, but the Africans were against it. The Federation brought great economic progress, including the building of the Kariba Dam. But in all three countries African political parties sought independence without European control and their freedom-fighting began in earnest in the form of guerrilla warfare. In Rhodesia it was fierce and prolonged against the white settlers wish to preserve their land, and it became known as The Bush War. The Rhodesian Front, a combination of the main white political parties, came to power in 1962. When the Federation was dissolved Rhodesia went back to being a British Colony. The White population then demanded independence for Rhodesia, since it had been granted to Zambia and Malawi, but the UK refused to permit independence without a guarantee of majority rule within a specified period. Therefore, in 1965, the Rhodesian Prime Minister, Ian Smith, issued a Unilateral Declaration of Independence (UDI). The United Nations and the UK were displeased. They called it rebellion and imposed sanctions on Rhodesia, but these did not stop the revolt, and in 1970 Rhodesia declared itself a republic. By 1975 the European population had reached 278,000. The economy had diversified. There were many successful commercial farmers. Exports included copper, asbestos, nickel, tobacco, cotton, gold, chrome, sugar tea and citrus fruit. There was also light industry such as the manufacture of biscuits and bicycles. Forestry and fishing were important too, with fish farming on Lake Kariba. It is worth mentioning that at this time more than 95% of African children attended primary schools, mainly mission schools. I do not know of any country in black

Africa that has ever reached this standard, and I am absolutely certain that none do now.

However, pressure on Rhodesia increased in intensity. Economic sanctions began to take their toll, and guerrilla warfare spread throughout the territory. Eventually Ian Smith was driven to capitulate. In 1978, following the intervention of the US diplomat Henry Kissinger and the UK, an agreement was reached on a transitional government leading to black majority rule. But there was no black unity in Rhodesia. Therefore a conference was held at Lancaster House in London 1979-80 where Lord Soames was appointed Governor to oversee the holding of elections. This brought to power the leader of the Zimbabwean African National Union, Robert Mugabe. Zimbabwe was granted independence under Mugabe in 1980.

There has always been a tradition of local arts and crafts in Zimbabwe. The people make traditional jewellery, baskets, textiles and pottery. Wood carving and sculpture are both practised. Shona sculpture is mainly stylised figures carved out of soft rock such as soapstone. These products were sold to tourists, but nowadays there is less than a trickle of tourists to Zimbabwe.

Provision for education is good though access to it is difficult. Government Schools are free in Zimbabwe but there are so many charges attached to school enrolment that many people cannot afford them. Independent schools are flourishing still, with white teachers among the staff, and these are where the wealthy portion of the population send their children. Higher education in Zimbabwe for those who can afford it is excellent. There are seven public universities plus four church related universities that are fully internationally accredited. According to an article in Wikipedia Zimbabwean trained doctors, for instance, only require one year of residence to be fully licensed doctors in the United States. However, these educational privileges are only open to rich people who can pay in United States dollars, a minuscule proportion of the population. The Zimbabwean dollar is almost worthless.

During the 1990s and the early years of the twenty first century President Mugabe's regime in Zimbabwe became progressively more corrupt and violent, and his behaviour and that of his followers, the war veterans, was bestial and abhorrent. Mugabe ruled Zimbabwe for three decades, and as a result he was soon ruling a country whose economy was in tatters, where poverty and unemployment were rampant, and discord and repression run of the mill.

Mugabe's Land Reform Programme – the seizure of most of the white-owned commercial farms was, according to Mugabe, for the benefit of landless black Zimbabweans – caused the collapse of agriculture, until then the basis of the economy. The legality of the process was often challenged by the High and Supreme courts in Zimbabwe but Mugabe and his cronies do not act in accordance with court rulings. Land redistribution led to a perilously sharp decline in agricultural exports, bringing about shortages of consumer goods and fuel. Many thousands of Zimbabweans, including experienced professionals, emigrated at this stage. Many more survived on food handouts. International opinion was now full of condemnation for the people it had, by insistence on black majority rule, thrust into power.

In 2002 Zimbabwe was suspended from the Commonwealth on charges of election rigging and human rights abuses. Also legislation in 2001 prohibited any efforts to extend loans, credit, or debt cancellation to the Zimbabwean government, leaving the territory in financial isolation. The legislation was put in place because all aid given to Zimbabwe went straight into the pockets of Mugabe and his supporters who dictated the country with a repressive and brutal regime. The current humanitarian crisis is the worst since independence.

There was more international condemnation when Mugabe, in 2005, demolished the urban slums, calling them 'illegal structures' and claiming it was necessary to keep law and order. Many of them housed opposition supporters. Either way, it left around 700,000 people homeless and jobless.

During 2008 there was a move to bring white farmers back, but much of the land that had been taken from them was no longer productive. Some started again, but then the government changed its mind and demanded all white farmers to leave the country or face jail.

The first real challenge to Mugabe's rule came during 2008 from the opposition Movement for Democratic Change, the MDC under the guidance of Morgan Tczangarai. Members of this party were beaten, tortured, harassed and killed by Mugabe's supporters. There is no freedom of speech in Zimbabwe and foreign media are not allowed in. However, some managed to infiltrate from South Africa, and the pictures of victims of torture shown on British television during the spring of 2008 were horrific.

One could only admire the tenacity of the MDC, and its persistence in continuing the struggle to remove Mugabe from his position of dictator. Mugabe accused the opposition party of being a tool of Western powers. An election was held in March 2008 that was by no means free and fair. Nevertheless, the MDC won it by two votes. This was disputed by the president, and publication of the results was delayed for over a month. Mugabe then went for a re-run in June, when he was the only contender. Murders and violent attacks on opposition supporters were increased to the extent that Morgan Tczangarai pulled out to prevent any more sickening assaults on his followers.

Eventually, after the intervention of the ex President of South Africa, Thabo Mbeki, with whom Mugabe agreed to talk, an arrangement was made to accept Tczangarai as prime minister, but Mugabe remains president, and he has kept under his control, among other things, the army, the police, and Home Affairs, and Tczangarai claims there is no power sharing.

At the time of writing this nobody knows what the eventual outcome will be. But we do know that right now large numbers of Zimbabweans are starving. They are trying to live on berries, and roots they dig up from the ground. Unless international aid is forthcoming there may soon be a major human disaster. This situation was inconceivable in Rhodesia.

The economy of Zimbabwe, with its supply shortages is now in a state of hyperinflation and the Central Statistical Office in

Zimbabwe estimated in November 2008 that the inflation rate was 516 quintillion per cent, with prices doubling every 1.3 days. Thus Zimbabwean money is useless for most purposes, and the currency in use by those who have access to them are American dollars, even though they are supposed to be illegal. The politicians themselves are clearly living in good conditions and are well-nourished. It follows they must have access to US money. The supply of weapons to the army and policing forces must also be supplied by some country or people supporting Mugabe.

The United Nations World Health Organisation has given the life expectancy of Zimbabwean men as 37 and of women as 34 years of age, one of the lowest in the world. The AIDS epidemic is partly responsible but poverty, the huge unemployment rate, shortage of food, lack of adequate sanitation and health care facilities are far more important issues.

Robert Mugabe is a violent, corrupt, amoral African dictator. He was the first President, and up until now (2008) the only one. His brutal and corrupt dictatorship presided over the collapse of Rhodesia's successful economy and the ruin of Zimbabwe.

Everybody knows that Mugabe must go but nobody knows how to remove the stubborn, outrageous, octogenarian president from power.

Ian Smith & The End of Rhodesia

The African colonies belong to past times, and Rhodesia is as dead as the dodo. Ian Smith had run a highly successful African country, with increasing prosperity among both whites and blacks. It had a booming and varied economy free from the post colonial scourge of corruption.

It is true Smith was a zealous supporter of white rule, and to his critics his government symbolised the worst of racial oppression. He was unrepentant. He had the ability to arouse strong emotion, and he was utterly hated by many for this unrepentant belief that white rule was better for everyone. If historians of the future mock Ian Smith, and dismiss him as a colonial caricature from another era, I hope you will challenge them with a different point of view.

For years it was a major producer of tobacco. Rhodesia was often called 'the bread basket of Africa'. There was also a small but thriving manufacturing industry producing goods of various kinds from clothes to food products to farm equipment to blankets and other commodities. There were productive fields of grain crops, there were cattle farms, there were orchards, and all sorts of fruit and vegetable growing.

All the services ran smoothly. Almost every child had at least primary education. There were schools, hospitals, clinics and sports facilities staffed by qualified people. It was a country that had everything going for it.

Is it any wonder the white settlers did not want to hand power over to the black politicians, certainly not at this time, when colonial powers were busy granting independence to black leaders in other African countries, and they had seen these other countries rapidly descend into dictatorship, violence, corruption, and poverty?

To them it seemed the West was only too willing to overlook these uncomfortable facts while condemning Rhodesians for not wanting to follow suit. Whatever its faults, Rhodesia offered stability, straightforward honesty, relative security and comparative prosperity to its citizens of all skin tones.

Ian Smith on one occasion was rash enough to say 'I don't believe in black majority rule over Rhodesia, not in a thousand years.' He managed to convince many white Rhodesians they could defy international opinion for ever, though some of us knew, unhappily, this was an unrealistic dream.

Rhodesia is dead. She died slowly, heinously strangled by international pressure, economic sanctions, and guerrilla warfare. Even South Africa, despite its own apartheid laws, threatened to withdraw support and thus cut off Rhodesia's lifeline.

Smith was forced to capitulate. He resigned as prime minister in January 1979, but a deal was made with the moderate black leaders under Muzorewa and his African National Congress party and he stayed on as minister without portfolio. Some seats in parliament were temporarily reserved for white politicians but the whites had already lost control.

It soon became obvious that the moderate black leaders were unable to stop the guerrilla campaign, and the Rhodesian armed forces were critically short of resources. In September 1979 Smith had to attend a peace conference at Lancaster House in London organised by the new British Prime Minister Margaret Thatcher, at which he conceded defeat.

As a result of this conference Rhodesia, for a very short time, became a British colony again. The British cabinet minister Lord Soames was appointed Governor to oversee Rhodesia's progress towards free and fair elections and majority rule. These elections took place in 1980 and Robert Mugabe's Zanu PF party won.

Rhodesia became Zimbabwe. Up until now this was the last time the people of Zimbabwe were free to vote for any party other than ZANU, a case of 'one man one vote – once.' Ian Smith remained in Zimbabwean politics until seats reserved for whites were abolished in 1987, after which he retired into the background, there to watch the subsequent total destruction of the sound, astutely managed, economically viable country he had fought so hard to preserve.

Ian Smith understood the unpalatable truths about Africa. He was a native of Rhodesia. He was born there, he grew up there amongst her people, black and white, he belonged there. Furthermore he, and most people who had lived in central Africa, including us, and who were interested in defending 'civilised standards', had witnessed so many dreadful things.

We had watched the flight of Belgian refugees from the Congo, we had been horrified by Idi Amin's brutality in Tanzania, we had observed the rise of a vicious and dysfunctional government in neighbouring Zaire, and we had seen the corruption and mismanagement in Zambia and Malawi immediately to the north of Rhodesia.

There was no reason to believe that Mugabe would be any different. In 1964 Smith had imprisoned Mugabe for 10 years for terrorist activities. This step was later condemned by those opposed to white rule as a racist act. It was not that simple. The banishment was for seriously inflammatory rhetoric and for violent and brutish behaviour against those who opposed his views, white or black.

Smith also imprisoned other black fanatics, sometimes ruthlessly, in order to protect his people from menacing attacks by rabble-rousers. It was important for him, and for others, to maintain law and order and reasonable behaviour. Nowadays we do exactly the same thing with terrorists in our own country, sometimes with far less evidence of their guilt. After his release from prison the evidence of his cruelty became even greater. In 1980 Mugabe was plotting the destruction of a group of black political enemies, the Matabele, and he later sent in Korean-trained troops to carry it out in a campaign of murder and torture. Somewhere between ten and twenty thousand innocent people were murdered, and many more were injured and disfigured. They were from the "wrong" tribe.

The bizarre thing is that after Mugabe took over Smith did not fade away, he grew in popularity and standing. As I said before, he belonged to Africa, and he liked and respected the run of the mill black Africans he knew so well. In retirement he lived in his house in Harare, next to the Cuban embassy, and after the death of his wife Janet he lived there on his own with just a cook, and very little security, yet nobody came along with a machette to kill him.

When Smith walked out in the streets of Harare Africans gathered round him to shake his hand and wish him well. They saw him as a great warrior, someone who fought for what he believed in and did not give up, and this they admired, as they admired their own tribal chiefs. He was certainly a fighter. When the British were fighting World War Two he joined the RAF. He crashed in a Hurricane over North Africa in 1943 and his face was so badly damaged he had to have it rebuilt, giving him a fixed stare and an expressionless appearance which encouraged his later enemies to call him frozen and humourless. He was soon back on duty as a fighter pilot, was shot down over the Alps, spent some months hiding in Italy, and then escaped through France to rejoin the RAF and keep fighting. No wonder he felt when he was fighting against the extinction of his own country that Britain betrayed him.

As Mugabe's regime became soaked in blood, turning more and more violent as time went by, Africans of every sort flocked to Ian Smith's house to seek advice from him, ask him what they should do. Sadly, there was nothing he could do to help them; he no longer had control over Mugabe's 'gangsters', as he always called them. He roundly condemned the corrupt and vicious regime, and when he publicly expressed this condemnation to the students at Zimbabwe University, all black, he was given a standing ovation.

To the end of his days Ian Smith nursed a sense of grievance about the way he had been 'betrayed' by the very countries he felt should have been his friends, Britain and South Africa. His war experiences in Europe left an enduring impression on him. Britain owed him. The fact that Rhodesia had done more than any other colony to help the British when they needed it added to his feeling of betrayal by post-war British governments. In his book, 'The Great Betrayal', published in 1997, he wrote 'During UDI we had the greatest national spirit in the world, a fantastic country,

great race relations, the happiest black faces in the world…
If our friends hadn't betrayed us we'd have won.'

But, as I said, there was nothing he could do. Within a
few years the predicted one-party state was established, the
economy was in ruins, and chaos reigned in Zimbabwe.

Ian Smith died on 22nd November 2007, aged 88. He
spent the last few years of his life in a residential home,
and he had recently had a stroke. He died in a clinic near
Cape Town. He died still believing he had been right. He
felt vindicated by the continuing crises in Zimbabwe and
its descent into hyperinflation, economic collapse, unemployment, general mayhem, and a population on the brink
of starvation. He was convinced that Rhodesians, black and
white, would have been better, happier and wealthier under
his leadership than that of Robert Mugabe.

A Tale of Zimbabwe 2008

To end my Facts about Zimbabwe notes let me tell you about
intrepid and wealthy survivors of the storms.

My friend John, the very John who was Information Officer
in Malawi in the 1960s and helped me to settle into colonial
life, has recently visited Zimbabwe. He is over 80 now and
lives in a comfortable, well-protected enclave in Cape Town,
but he is wholly Rhodesian. He was invited by the headmaster of a prestigious school in Harare to be guest speaker at the
school's 80th birthday celebration, a black tie dinner for some
200 people at Meikles Hotel, another expensive survivor of
the troubles. This school was started by John's father in 1928.
John and his wife, also Rhodesian, went. Both had relatives
and friends still in the country so there would be no shortage of hosts. The visit took place in November 2008, when
Robert Mugabe and Morgan Tsvangirai had failed to agree
about sharing of ministries, most schools and hospitals had
collapsed, and food was short. It was a hot, dry, and smoky
time of year just before the rains broke.

I will talk about the first household in which they stayed, but the pattern was repeated time and time again. The hosts had been prosperous white farmers who lost all three farms with everything on them. Some of their cattle were mutilated and killed. John described their present house as lovely, surrounded by Msasa trees, and with outbuildings which housed a gardener, a maid, and three others who helped with building work. The Municipal water supply had failed so they relied on rusty borehole water, plus water bought for drinking. For electricity they had a generator. A car battery was used for lights and TV, on which they could get BBC news. These systems were used by most white residents. Drinks and dinner were excellent. Petrol for the car was obtained from some backstreet. Everyone with US dollars seemed able to buy everything they needed, though they had to be resourceful.

The school celebration at Meikles was a great success. The three course dinner with abundance of South African wine was of international standard. John spoke of his connections with the school and of the lives of his parents. An auction raised 30,000 US dollars for a new tennis court at the school, and the guests danced the might away to a white band.

Afterwards more friends were visited, most with sad stories of stolen farms, brutality and forced eviction, but all with enough resources outside Zimbabwe to acquire US dollars on which they can live in the above-mentioned resourceful way. John asked one of them how they got on with the local Zimbabweans all around them. The reply was there had not been one spot of trouble. It seems there is very little, if any, anti white feeling and most of the populace want Mugabe 'out'.

John's last hosts had been allowed to return to part of their farm because the authorities planned to turn it into a training centre one day. The farmer found the land remaining to him was not big enough to run a viable commercial farm, and so he appropriated a bit of adjoining bush, ploughed it up and fertilised it, doing a similar piece of land for the African settlers. Now he had a workable patch of land to farm and he was running a successful business once more. He showed his visitors the granadilla fields and the large packing shed for granadillas waiting to be exported. His new modern tobacco barns were as they should be for the purpose, and he was providing jobs and shelter for several hundred Africans. John's visit to Zimbabwe came to an end on this working farm, so good to see, and the guests flew off in the farmer's Cessna aircraft heading for Harare Airport and a flight back to South Africa.

The preceding few paragraphs describing the continuation of white life in Zimbabwe is taken from a report on his visit sent to me by John Carver. Wow. There are still defiant, creative, resourceful, old-style Rhodesians refusing to leave their country. This leaves me with a positive feeling that Zimbabwe may yet rise from the present-day ruins and begin all over again.

There are Rhodesians, and descendents of Rhodesians, in many corners of the modern world for whom the bright flame lily, the national flower of Rhodesia, will for ever burn in hearts and minds.

Four

Roaming; 1964–65

December 1964

Dear Ruth,

We have moved. We are now in Lusaka. Our life in Nyasaland ended in September when the new Malawi Government took over the Ministry of Posts, which was Jim's Ministry. We went to wonderful Salisbury for a short time, as most federal civil servants did, while we made a decision about what to do next. There were jobs on offer in all three of the former federal territories, so we had three choices:

1. *To stay where we were and to work for the Government of Malawi.*

2. *To move to Southern Rhodesia, about to become just Rhodesia.*

3. *To move to Northern Rhodesia, soon to become Zambia.*

Other things being equal, the obvious choice would have been to go for Rhodesia because it is a cultured, civilised, well-developed country, with all the usual amenities we expect to find in Europe, and with the big plus of a good climate and easy living. It was a self-governing British Colony before the creation of the Federation of Rhodesia and Nyasaland in 1953, and now it has reverted to a British colony, and is still governed by the 'Whites'. As an ex federal civil servant Jim would probably have been offered a job there. But I would not, and I wanted a job too. I would find it difficult to settle for being identified as 'the wife' of somebody else. Rhodesia provides first-class education for its citizens right up to university level and beyond, and it has plenty of home-grown social workers. It would neither want nor need to take on a British ex-colonial civil servant. Northern Rhodesia, on the other hand, still employs a large number of expatriates on attractive salaries, and is likely to do so for some time to come. Thus we took choice three, to move to Northern Rhodesia.

Accordingly, here we are. The conditions of work are much the same as they were in Nyasaland, including a Government house furnished with basic furniture. We brought with us our large supply of domestic equipment, most of which we shall never use in this country because lavish entertaining is only an expectation from staff with senior posts, and I am unlikely to get one of those. Married women have to follow their husbands from place to place and take what jobs are on offer in situ. Sometimes there are none. The house we have been allocated is the usual government bungalow. It is in a pleasant area called Woodlands, with an English-style pub, The Woodpecker, just a short walk away. The Woodpecker serves simple pub meals such as Chicken-in-a-Basket and Fish and Chips and we sometimes go there for a cheap evening out. Most of our neighbours are British. We have two energetic domestic servants to look after the domestic chores, so life is really quite comfortable. Nevertheless, Willard and John in Nyasaland will be sadly missed because they were quite exceptional, and made me the envy of my friends and colleagues.

Lusaka is an agreeable town with plenty of amenities. It is nice to be able to go to the shops and buy what one needs, and to drive along properly engineered tar roads. Also the political situation here is far more acceptable, at least at the present time. There is freedom of speech, and a free press, and no great 'Saviour' such as Banda, to whom all must bow down and worship. You will have heard about the recent general election here which put the United National Independence Party into power with a big majority. Party Members have now taken over the Government under Kenneth Kaunda and it remains to be seen what they will do with their power. Kaunda seems to be a reasonable, fairly moderate sort of person. The question is, will he be able to control his minions? Certainly neither he nor they will tolerate any opposition to their Party's rule. There is a good deal of fear amongst the European population that this place will go the same way as so many other African States. Frankly, I think it will, but at the moment life is very pleasant so we might as well enjoy it while we can. At least Northern Rhodesia is a relatively wealthy territory. Quite apart from the Copper Mines, which are flourishing, so many European firms have invested interests here and they are not going to back out in a hurry.

Independence Day came along soon after we arrived. It was on 24th October, and we went to the ceremony. The stadium was packed and the cheering Africans were noisy and raucous, although they did calm down for the solemnity of the hand-over. The Princess Royal, old Princess Alice, represented the Queen, and there were various other British dignitaries on the rostrum, together with Kenneth Kaunda and a large collection of Zambian politicians. The moment came. The Union Jack was slowly lowered and the Zambian flag raised, followed by a hullabaloo as it fluttered in the breeze.

It was not difficult for me to get a job here, and I am now working as a Social Welfare Officer in the Lusaka District Office. The work is quite arduous, but it is interesting and varied, covering just about every possible branch of social work At least I am not in charge of anything important and I don't have to control a budget or allocate any scarce resources. We have adequate money and other facilities to help us along the way, though I rather fear things might change when the new Government really gets going. The Officer-in-Charge of Lusaka District is called Bill, and under him he has three social workers, all women, two of us are British and one a white South African. Most civil servants of moderate seniority are still white, with black messengers, drivers, clerks, and so forth. Our clients come from all sections of the community, black, coloured, Asian, European, and others. A lot of the work is concerned with child care, prison after care, disabled people, probation work, and public assistance in the form of food vouchers which can be exchanged in shops. There are more Europeans in all sorts of trouble hereabouts than there were in Nyasaland. Some of the farmers who came here from the south are not making a success of their farms, and there are few jobs here for unskilled whites. The children of such people tend not to go to school so they also finish up unskilled. We try to send them back to South Africa where more help is available but most seem happy to muddle along here. But of course the majority of people who come to us are African.

We have been having some excitement in the office just recently because of the rebellion of Alice Lenshina and her Lumpa Church in the north of the country. I expect it was recorded in British newspapers. Lumpa means 'better than all others'. This Church opposes any earthly authority and it openly challenged Kenneth Kaunda and the UNIP. Needless to say Kaunda used force to suppress this challenge. Alice Lenshina convinced her followers that they are protected by God, and the weapons of the army and the police would not harm them. They went out with bows and arrows to defend themselves, and their defeat resulted in the death of 700 church members during police and army attacks. Added to this, many people were badly injured, so Bill, our boss, was sent to the north to deal with the sick and the wounded, and he sent them to Lusaka for us to deal with. Thus we had an emergency change in routine while one or other of us handled the problems. We arranged for most of them to be admitted to hospital and visited them there to record as many details about them as we could. It took a long time. The survivors will eventually have to be sent back to their villages, and they will need to toe the Party line.

Thank you for your advice to me as a newly-wed. I will bear your wisdom in mind but in fact, yes, I am enjoying married life, and actually we have lived in harmony right from the beginning. Perhaps the difficulties of which you speak are yet to come. Just now we both have busy lives outside the home and therefore nothing much has changed. Socially we had been doing most things together for well over a year before we were married. We had to learn to live together, but it was not a problem.

Jim is working very hard just now. The Ministry of Posts is suffering from an acute shortage of staff due to the break up of the Federation and the flight of most of the members of staff from their unpopular northern postings to the golden land of Rhodesia, from where many of them came. The result is that all leave has been stopped for the time being. We were due for long leave in UK this year (six months), but we could not possibly get away before the end of the year, and what is the point of visiting Europe in the winter? Our tentative plans now are to leave here next March, fly to Europe for a short holiday on the Continent, and then on to Britain for the summer. Jim will be due for seven months leave by then. After that we plan to return to Africa, possibly sailing from Italy by the East Coast sea route and bringing a new car back with us on the ship.

However, it is difficult to make definite arrangements at this stage. Until May 1965 Jim is still officially seconded to the Northern Rhodesian Government from the ex Federal Government. He then plans to sign on with the Zambian Government, but at the moment we cannot easily predict what the situation will be. There will almost certainly be a job for him, but he can be posted to any place in the country, and where it might be is anyone's guess. This means that, sadly, I shall have to resign from my job in Lusaka. It will be like starting over again.

The uncertainty about our future whereabouts may help to settle one issue. Regretfully, I can no longer call myself a free spirit, dancing through my twenties with no set ideas about what I might do next. Having no job to come back to will give me time to consider the options. I am now 30 years old. Oh dear. Perhaps we should be thinking about whether or not we want a family. Interested friends ask personal questions about it, and I tell them there is plenty of time for that, but perhaps there no longer is.

Anyway, first things first. I am looking forward to 1965, and the freedom to do as we wish for half a year. Basically we shall use it for visiting friends and relatives, and to travel around our own country, going to places we have never had time to visit before. We hope to call in on you while we are in England, if you are at home at the right time, and we look forward to that.

April 1965

Dear Ruth,

Yes, we were granted our seven months home leave, with the promise of a job for Jim when we return to Zambia in September. The ex-federal government gave us return air fares to London, and we can use the money as we like. Hence I am writing this letter in England. We left Lusaka in March *on a flight to Heathrow. We had already bought a new car, a Ford Corsair in a pale shade of yellow, and we arranged for it to be at Heathrow to meet us. We are delighted with the car and we hope it will serve us well for some time to come. We drove it into London and parked it in Earls Court, where we rented a room, and we stopped there for a week or two using this room as a base. We went to Gloucestershire and stayed for a few days with my widowed mother, visiting a few people around and about. It was the place where I grew up during the war. In London, apart from taking advantage of what London has to offer, we visited Jim's separated parents in the East End, and his brother and family in Brixton. Now that family visits have been done we can go anywhere we like, and it gives us a great feeling of freedom. But I had forgotten about the appalling British weather. It is supposed to be spring but so far we have experienced nothing but dark skies and cold wet days, and there are occasions when I wish we had chosen to spend our leave exploring other parts of Africa. However, we decided on Britain, and we started off in Cornwall because we thought it would be the warmest place. We headed for Penzance, gazed across the grey sea at Lands End, and had a look at various other places in Cornwall, and then proceeded to Devon. We are chiefly using Bed and Breakfast accommodation the quality of which varies enormously, particularly when it comes to bathroom use. The landladies, though, are mostly kind and helpful. While we were in London we bought a book called Europe on Five $s a Day and this is helping us to find some comfortable but cheap places to stay. Now we are in Dorset, in the region of Lulworth, where there is a lovely coastal path, and places for brave people to camp in soggy fields. We walked a short distance along the path but nothing is very appealing in these dismal climatic conditions. We shall try again if it clears up. Meanwhile, this is our chance to come to see you in Blandford Forum. I hope you are not away, and this will be possible. There is no way you can contact us while we are moving* *about, but we shall move from here tomorrow and find a place to stay not too far away, then I will ring you to try to arrange a mutually convenient date and time.*

September 1965

Dear Ruth,

It was wonderful to see you in the spring and to catch up with your news. Your little girls are no longer little, and they are charming.

Now our long leave is nearly over and we are heading back to Zambia. At the moment we are staying with friends in Rhodesia and it is marvellous to be in a sunny climate again. I am sitting beside their swimming pool with plenty of time to write to you. You said you love to get my letters, and you asked me to let you know what we did during all those weeks we were on leave. Do you really want a travelogue of our experiences? What we did was to travel from place to place like gipsies, visiting as many places as we could fit into the time available. Well, here it is. I will try to be brief, but we did a lot of things.

After we left you in Dorset we went on to Hampshire, through the New Forest, and then to Oxford and Buckinghamshire, occasionally staying with friends, but mostly using our B&B book. Somewhere around here we branched off west to Wales. We went to Three Cocks near Brecon where Jim spent his time as an evacuee in the 1940s, and we visited his former foster mother, now very old. A child who was boarded in the same home at the time was drowned one winter's day by falling through the ice on the River Wye. He is buried in the local churchyard in a grave with the simple inscription 'Tommy..., London Evacuee, aged 11.' But the nice thing is that the grave has been carefully tended over the years, and there was a fresh bunch of flowers in a pretty bowl on the top. We continued through Wales to Pembrokeshire, took a long and very pretty walk along the coast from Tenby to Saundersfoot, then went inland, had a look at Mount Snowdon shrouded in mist, and roamed around other parts of Wales.

After Wales we headed for the Midlands, visiting friends along the way. We stayed for a few days in Stratford on Avon, where we went to see one of Shakespeare's plays at the Shakespeare Memorial Theatre, and we toured around the tourist sites, and tried canoeing on the river, an activity that was unpleasantly wet. From there we travelled north on the west side of England, through Cheshire and into Lancashire. Crossing the Mersey from Runcorn to Widnes was exceedingly disagreeable. That part of Lancashire was full of factory chimneys belching black smoke and we didn't hang around for too long, although Formby and Southport were nice enough places. We went on to the Lake District, paid tribute to Wordsworth at Dove Cottage, and stayed beside Lake Windermere while we explored the area. We found it very beautiful but also very wet. We had some squelchy walks in the hills, and discovered the delight of cold Kit Kat bars sold from machines scattered around the district. From Cumberland we crossed over to the east into Northumberland, and then to Durham and York, staying for a few days in both these pleasant and interesting cities. We had a wander around Bronte country, visited Haworth parsonage and walked on the Yorkshire moors, which I found cold, windy and bleak, although a dog-walking Yorkshireman we met on the way described them as 'grand and fresh', and both he and the dog were clearly having a great time.

Next we travelled south on the eastern side of the country, passing through Lincolnshire and into East Anglia. We drove by the Norfolk Broads, and had a brief look at the Norfolk and Suffolk coastlines. Along the way we visited a good many Stately Homes run by the National Trust, the names and history of which soon faded into oblivion. In almost every town we went to the town museum. Jim loves museums and can spend much time marvelling at relics from our historic past.

By now the time had come to start on Scotland, and we made this journey on a sleeper train. We drove to Ely, put the car on the train, clambered into our sleeping compartment, and slept all the way to Stirling. Thus we arrived in Scotland fresh to begin our exploration north of the border. It was cold, even colder than the north of England, though by then we were well into June. We went to Perth, then on to the fine city of Edinburgh, dominated by the castle perched atop the crags of an ancient volcano.

We stayed in Edinburgh for several days. The wind from the east was bitter but nontheless we enjoyed exploring the ancient Royal Mile, the winding medieval streets, and the modern Princes Street, bordered on the south side by the Castle Rock and beautiful gardens, and on the northern side by many shops and offices. The shops, among other things, all sold whisky, shortbread and tartan.

From Edinburgh we travelled north on the west side of the country which is said to have a mild climate, but it has not. It has, however, splendid scenery with deep valleys dominated by mountains. We were on our way to Inverness, and decided to go to the Highland Show which was held on midsummer day, but when we arrived there I refused to get out of the car because it was snowing, yes snowing. A rather nasty sleety sort of snow, and it was freezing cold. Jim had a brief look at the cattle and then we proceeded to Inverness. The weather improved, and we really liked Inverness and stayed there for a while in a modest little hotel near to the River Ness. Being that far north in mid summer gave us very long evenings and it was fun to walk along the river bank until after ten and still have daylight. As well as enjoying the busy little city with its interesting streets and buildings we made various excursions into neighbouring places of interest. We drove around Loch Ness, visited the site of the Battle of Culloden, and went to Aviemore in the Cairngorms.

After Inverness we made our way to Fort William, and then over the sea to Skye. In Skye we had warm weather, a big bonus in this abysmal summer. The sun shone warmly and the sky was a gentle blue. We wandered in the sun, the warmth seeping into our bodies, and it was very enjoyable despite a plague of little black midges. The pleasure of getting some sunshine made us think that it was time to end our British touring and go to a place that was warm. Thus we set off for London, stopping at various points of interest on the way south, until we eventually arrived in Southend on the Essex coast. Southend had nothing to recommend it except an aeroplane to France on which we could take the car. Off we went to Paris.

The first thing I noticed when we drove into the heart of Paris was the traffic, and a gendarme, small in stature, guiding a multitude of moving cars around the Arc de Triomphe. I decided that driving in Paris was not for me, though Jim was a lot braver. However, we mostly explored on foot, and we saw all the usual things a visitor to Paris might like to see. I had been there before but Jim had not. Paris is dominated by the River Seine, along the banks of which we walked many times as we visited the various districts. Anyone who reads these notes will know Paris. We had a look round Notre Dame Cathedral, spent an hour or two in the Louvres, looked at the shops in the Champs Elysees, and climbed the Eiffel Tower. We particularly enjoyed the district around the Sacre Coeur, where several artists sat painting. We also spent an interesting day at the Palace of Versailles.

Paris was a good experience, but the weather was similar to London and we still had not found the warmth I was craving for. On 1st August we set off for the south of France, and in Nice there was the sun, hot and smiling, but getting there presented unexpected obstacles. We did not know that the first two weeks in August were holiday weeks for vast numbers of French workers, and every single one of them seemed to be on the motorway heading for the French Riviera. The road was solid with traffic that hardly moved. We bore with it for a while, then branched off into the French Alps and took a long and leisurely drive through the hills, stopping at a very pleasant guest house for the night, where we were provided with a delicious meal, eaten alfresco looking out across wonderful mountain views.

Nice, Cannes, Monaco. These places were packed with holiday-makers enjoying the sun. The weather was perfect, and this was such a bonus after months of cool, damp, and gloomy days, but I didn't find anything of abiding interest about the French Riviera. From Monaco we travelled on along the coast heading for Italy, another slow, traffic-logged journey with overnight stops on the way, but in due course we arrived.

The highlights of our touring in Italy were the cities of Rome, Florence and Venice, with a brief visit to Pisa to see the leaning tower. I am a townie rather than a country person, and find old cities fascinating, and I was especially captivated by Rome, with its relics of classical times. We wandered amongst the ruins of the Forum, the Pantheon and the Coliseum, and walked up and down ancient streets lined with statues and Roman columns. We also viewed what we could of the Vatican, threw coins in the fountain near the Basilica of St Peter, and joined the bustle in the more modern parts of Rome. The crowning glory of Rome for us was the most wonderful production of Aida performed in the open air at the Coliseum.

We found Florence full of fine buildings and beautiful bridges, as well as churches, art galleries and museums. As you know, it is one of the greatest artistic centres of the world. We went to many of the galleries, including the Uffizi and the Pitti Palace, and they were full of fantastic things, but after a while we became satiated with so many works of art and were glad to move on to Venice, travelling up the Adriatic coast which we found more attractive than the Mediterranean.

Venice rises out of the water. There were no proper streets to drive along, and we joined everybody else, travelling by boat along the canals, either by ferry boat, or in a gondola propelled by one oarsman, the gondolier. We used both methods. It seemed to me a novel idea and I enjoyed it, but would not like to live with the arrangement. Jim hated water transport and this coloured his view of Venice, which is in fact a very beautiful city. The Grand Canal was alive with boats. As our boat zigzagged from stop to stop the city unfolded, with palaces, churches and views down side canals. One beautiful building followed another, the water lapping against them. The boat went under the Rialto Bridge, passed the city's art gallery, and as we approached the end of the Grand Canal we saw the superb Ducal Palace facing open water. We got off the boat and made our way to St Mark's Square, and this will be my most enduring memory of Venice. All around were cafes with tables outside in the square. Many of them had orchestras playing, and sitting there in the sun drinking gins and tonic and watching people coming and going was sheer delight. We moved on to the sea port of Trieste. Here we boarded an Italian ship called the Europa, which would take us on the east coast route back to Africa. Jim's father Bill joined us at this stage, for a holiday, which was a mistake as it turned out because he had a gastric ulcer and was unwell for most of the time. Days at sea were much the same as they are on any sea voyage, but the glory of the Europa was that it had plenty of stops along the way where one could get off the boat and explore.

As always, the sea air seemed to increase appetites and most of the passengers were preoccupied by food, possibly enhanced by endless games of deck quoits. There were a lot of Germans on the ship and one small thing I shall always remember was a fight between the Germans and the English over cakes at tea time. They seemed to be lined up against one another as if they were still fighting World War Two. The contest was about who would get at the cakes first, and who could grab the most. Elbows were poked into ribs, hands tugged and pulled, and one Englishman made a fist as if he intended to land a punch. I stood back and choked with laughter in an undignified way. Eventually calm was restored.

The ship's first stop was Brindizi, on the heal of Italy, to load and unload goods, and we went into the town and had a look round but there was nothing special about it. Then we went on to Port Said. Here we joined a group on an excursion to Cairo by coach while the ship made its slow way through the Suez Canal. We were taken to Giza to view the sphinx and the pyramids, where we wandered about, refused to ride on a camel, but climbed inside a pyramid. One had to admire the astonishing feats of ancient engineering, though the tombs had been robbed long-ago. After that we were taken for lunch at a restaurant in Cairo. We did not see much of the city, but a few of us visited the Egyptian Museum to see the treasures of ancient Egypt, including the finds from the tomb of Tutankhamun. Then we made the long journey to Suez and were put into a small boat that bobbed around on the Red Sea as we waited for our ship to emerge from the canal. Before long it loomed into view and, although the Europa was a relatively small ship, it looked massive as it approached our little boat. We were hauled on board.

We proceeded to sail along the Red Sea to Djibouti, where we stopped for a while, and then travelled on through the Indian Ocean along the East Coast of Africa. Ports of call on the way included Mogadishu, Mombassa and Dar es Salaam, and we were allowed on shore at each one. The natives always gathered beside the ship selling their wares, and we bought a wall carpet at Mogadishu which will hang on the wall of our next house. I particularly enjoyed Mombassa. It was very hot, and I walked along the beach with bare feet, the sand running warmly through my toes as we headed for a group of basket-making locals. Eventually we arrived at Beira in Portuguese East Africa, where we disembarked. We were meant to go straight to a large game reserve called Gora Gora, pre-booked and paid for, but Bill was too unwell to cope with this so we had to push on to Umtali in Rhodesia to find a good doctor. Bill was amazed to find that the doctor had trained at Guys Hospital, very close to home. He was given medication, and after a short stay we drove north to the fine city of Salisbury, and here we are. Bill's gastric ulcer stopped giving trouble, but then he complained of severe constipation, so again a doctor was called to give appropriate treatment. It was with some relief that we put him on a plane back to London.

End of travelogue. Our seven months leave is over and tomorrow we set off for Lusaka and Jim's next posting. Where will it be? We shall soon find out.

Abercorn 1965

Dear Ruth,

When we arrived back in Lusaka news of our postings was waiting for us. We had two. To begin with Jim was to work in Abercorn for three months to cover for Giffard, the engineer who normally filled this post, while he went on three months leave. After that we were to go to Ndola. We stayed in a rather nasty government hostel in Lusaka for a few days before we set off for Abercorn. It was called Longacres. There were bed bugs in my mattress and they made me look as if I had impetigo.

Abercorn was bad news for me, extremely bad news, and only the fact that it was a temporary placement made the notion bearable. It is a tiny place tucked away in the far north of Zambia near to the border with the Congo. In my view we were being sent out to the Bush, a place where there were no useful things to do, nowhere in particular to go, few shops, no tennis club, no anything. There would be a handful of Europeans to keep the services up and running, and possibly their wives. No jobs for wives. I imagined they would have made attractive gardens, and that they occupied themselves with domestic affairs. A boring group of 'nice' ladies. I soon discovered that I was absolutely right.

We made the long journey to Abercorn. Our belongings remained in store in Lusaka but the car was loaded with goodies we had acquired in Europe, and a few cans of petrol because there would not be much in the way of petrol stations en route. In fact we ran out of petrol on the way up. We had not made allowance for the fact that a heavily laden car uses more petrol than one that is carrying little. We managed to get to a rest house at a place called Mpika, and somebody went to find petrol for us. We set off again. In due course we arrived at Giffard's house in Abercorn and unpacked our bits and pieces. His servant, who was supposed to look after the domestic side of things, was an almost total disaster. He could not cook, and was lazy and incompetent, but clearly he suited Giffard and his wife so we could do nothing about it.

Abercorn was much as I expected, a dump. Yet there were a couple of shops and one could buy essentials such as meat, fish, vegetables, fruit, and basic groceries. We went shopping and came back with, among other things, a chicken and some vegetables. These I handed to the boy and asked him to cook dinner for us. He did, but he had failed to put his hands inside the chicken and pull out the insides! Now I had a task to do in Abercorn. I would do the cooking, and since I had not yet

developed any cooking skills I would have to learn. I acquired
a cookery book from one of the nice ladies, and I soon learned
that if you could read you could cook, although making meals
never grabbed my imagination. Preparing food and cooking it
was, and is, always a disagreeable chore, although Giffard's
servant could, after a fashion, do some of the preparation and
all of the clearing up. As it turned out, becoming proficient at
cooking was going to come in handy as the years rolled on.
Our previous house, in Woodlands, Lusaka, was the last one
in which we employed two capable servants and were able to
forget about household tasks. Life in Abercorn was not rosy, but
I met people who seemed content to be there. They had become
accustomed to living quiet, humdrum and unstimulating
lives, and I obtained some enjoyment by pondering over what
made them tick. There was a pub called the Abercorn Arms
where we could go to meet the neighbours for a drink and
social conversation. This was the nearest thing to a club that
existed. We had one very exciting night there on the day Ian
Smith made his Unilateral Declaration of Independence for
Rhodesia. This was on 11th November. The rejoicing amongst
the Europeans appeared to be unanimous, and we drank toasts
to Rhodesia, to Ian Smith, to the settlers who had made the
country what it is, and to the Rhodesian people, that they may
continue to prosper. The evening ended with us all dancing
in a circle outside singing 'We are marching to Rhodesia,
Rhodesia, Rhodesia. We are marching to Rhodesia, Rhodesia
HURAH.' Then we proceeded to dance a conga in the street,
and some laughing, good-humoured Africans joined in. So
much excitement, so much hope, yet many of us knew that in
the end it was doomed to go pear-shaped.

While we were in Abercorn I was summoned to Lusaka to
appear in a court case against one of my ex-colleagues. I
knew nothing about the circumstances of the case because
it happened while we were away on leave. I could only give
an excellent character reference, and this I did. For me it

was a useful interlude, and a welcome break from Abercorn. I travelled to Lusaka on a little propeller driven plane that bumped and bounced through the sky, flying low, until some of us were using our sick bags. I went to stay with friends in Lusaka for a couple of nights. The court case was over by lunch time the following morning. We won. Then I had a free afternoon to wander along Cairo Road, the main street in Lusaka. It had never before looked so pleasing. Suddenly I remembered I had a minor problem, and the doctor I had seen when we lived here was only a few steps away. My periods were always very erratic and if they stopped for too long this doctor gave me pills to bring them back. I walked into the surgery and told him they had stopped again.

"Let me just examine you," said he, "Hop on the table."

"Mmm. What would you say if I told you that you may be pregnant?"

I had not even thought of that. I looked at myself, reed-thin, with a stomach as flat as a board.

"I don't think I am" I assured him.

He asked for a specimen and told me to come back at the end of the afternoon.

That is how I discovered I was expecting my first child, and the baby was due at the beginning of June. Three months pregnant. I was surprised at how thrilled I felt, and at how easy it had been, since it must have happened immediately after Jim and I decided to let nature take its uninterrupted course.

The next day I returned to Abercorn. Jim was excited about the news I brought back with me, but also somewhat apprehensive. We both knew that becoming parents would change our lives for ever. By now we were nearing the end of our time in Abercorn. It passed by uneventfully, and shortly before Christmas we moved to Ndola.

Five

Ndola 1966–1968

January 1966

Dear Ruth,

A Happy New Year to you and the family. I hope you had a jolly Christmas, and that 1966 will bring all things good.

Jim has now officially signed a three-year-contract with the Zambian Government and his long term posting is here in Ndola, on the copper belt. We expect to be here until 1969. As you know, his employment with the Federal Government officially ended in September at the end of our Home Leave, and now we no longer have the comfortable backing of a federal government sitting in Salisbury. Oh dear. We are entirely at the mercy of the Zambians and nobody knows how their government will evolve. We do not think they are yet ready to run a western style economy. I can understand why the British at home take a more democratic view. You probably visualise a government with western values and ideals and competent politicians running the country along British lines. The only difference would be that those in charge are black Africans because they are the most numerous, the black majority, as Wilson reiterates time and time again like a gramophone record stuck on one tune. Believe me, the Africans are different in more ways than skin colour. They have a different culture, different ways of looking at life, different methods of doing things, and it's hard to imagine them running the country efficiently and democratically. I guess their rule will be more despotic in character, but we shall see.

You know that I am expecting a baby in June, and that is something to look forward to with delight, but also some trepidation. It came as a surprise, though perhaps it should not have done. I still can't quite believe it, and neither can anyone else, apart from the doctor who assures me this is so. I don't look pregnant and I don't feel pregnant: no weight gain, no sickness, and no expanding abdomen. Thus I have doubts every time I go to the antenatal clinic and sit amongst women with bellies sticking out like pumpkins, moaning one to the other about this ache, that pain, and horrid amounts of vomiting, and proudly dressed in pretty, voluminous maternity frocks. Perhaps I should buy a maternity dress? I do not feel that I belong to this group, but I'll let you know how it goes.

We are now settling down to life in Ndola. We were given a Government flat in Cecil Court within easy walking distance of the centre of town. It only has two bedrooms but one of them is colossal, and it will make a very useful nursery. We have never lived in a flat before, but this block is full of young couples, some of them with children, and we all get on very well together. Two of the women are also pregnant and one of these has a baby due at the same time as me. They are mostly teachers sent out by the British Government as part of an Aid Programme, and they are recruited and paid by the Crown Agents, a new body set up to take on some of the functions of the old colonial office. They are a different breed of expatriates from the long-term civil servants we are used to working alongside, who expected to stay in Africa for the rest of their lives, and probably retire here too. These new ones have all recently arrived, and are on time-limited contracts, home based in England, Scotland, or Ireland. They see their role in Africa through the eyes of British politicians. For instance, our neighbours Elsbeth and Jim, who came here from Eire, commented, with wide-open judgmental eyes that the white settlers are so arrogant they call their servants 'boys', although they are grown men, and they even summon them by ringing a bell! Goodness me, we shall have to be circumspect about what we say, at least to begin with, but later on I see scope for interesting discussion. They all employ a boy now, (whoops!) a man, to do the housework and the washing and ironing, the same as we do. Our servant is called Byson, a family man with lots of children. He comes every day at 6.00 a.m. and does all the household chores apart from cooking. Nowadays I have to cook for myself, but I had plenty of practice in Abercorn.

Ndola itself is a relatively small town but most of the necessities are available. Supplies are brought in from Rhodesia at the moment, crossing the border in Livingstone. British economic sanctions against Ian Smith and his government may affect these supplies in the near future. It is an agreeable but functional place to live, with an excellent climate. All the copper belt towns are nearby, and there are plenty of pleasant places to visit without having to travel far. An English-style pub called The Bull and Bush, with a lake and attractive gardens, is on the outskirts of the town, and close at hand are other enjoyable parks and retreats. We shall be happy to settle here for the next three years or so.

For 'personal reasons', as they say, I did not apply for a social work post in Ndola, but I have found a temporary part-time job managing the office for a very small firm called Bailey's Roofing. What I lack in typing skills I make up for by being charming to the clients, friendly and encouraging on the phone, and keeping files tidy and accounts sent out at specified times. They are happy to leave the administrative work to me while they go off and fix roofs, and it keeps me busy. I shall continue to do overseas home assessments for English Adoption Societies who want to place children with expatriates out here.

On the social side, we still play tennis. Ndola has no general-purpose European Club of the type to which we are accustomed. There is a Golf Club, a Squash Club, a Bridge Club, a Tennis Club, and various other special interest groups. Of course we joined the tennis club, and that is the main focus of our social life. This club has a bar that is open daily, a swimming pool, and a place to socialise both inside and out. You don't have to play tennis in order to join, though we still play tennis regularly.

We will let you know how the rest of the year evolves. Watch this space.

October 1966

Dear Ruth,

All came to pass as predicted. The baby eventually made his presence felt by kicking and squirming around and creating a hump in my stomach, quite a small hump, and I never did buy that maternity dress. Everybody told me it would be a very small baby, and, remarked one of the midwives, this was because I was an elderly prima para, older than I should be to have a first baby. Laurence James Cotton was born on 8th June and weighed in at a perfectly normal 7lbs. But why did you not tell me that childbirth is so horrendously painful? It was excruciating, the worst pain in the entire world.

Laurence is flourishing, and he is such a happy little thing. You would love him. He started to laugh when he was only four weeks old and has hardly stopped laughing since. Here he is when he was still very new:

Now we have moved on, and it is October. Laurence is forging ahead in leaps and bounds and he has recently become mobile by bumping his four month old body all round the nursery floor on his back. He is a very co-operative baby, praise be. He started sleeping through the night before he was six weeks old, aided

Pam, Jim & Laurence – July 1966, age 5 weeks

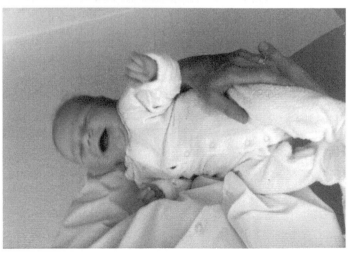

Laurence – July 1966, age 5 weeks

by a small spoonful of baby cereal stirred into his last bottle at the end of the day. By the time he was three months I had him on a nice convenient three-meals-a-day routine. Physically he is now 24 inches long and weighs 15 pounds. Quite a buster!

Yes, I am truly delighted with our little son, but nevertheless I do not find him all-absorbing. I am still doing the odd home study on prospective adopters living out here, but this is spasmodic. Thus I began to look around for something else to do. There are a number of other British social workers in Ndola who are not gainfully employed and between us we are now in the process of forming a voluntary personal service organisation. We envisage a kind of cross between the Citizens' Advice Bureau and the Samaritans. There are one or two legal formalities to be completed but we hope to get it going towards the end of this month. We have acquired an office in the M.O.T.H. (memorable order of tin hats) building which we are planning to man on three or four evenings a week to begin with. We have a very long list of prospective helpers who we will train to do the 'manning'. We have just completed a survey of local resources here, i.e. Red Cross, Save the Children, Rotary, W.V.S., Salvation Army etc. It was interesting to find out what they all do. Now we are making a card index of them for future reference. Laurence travels around with me for most of the time, and seems to enjoy it, and my colleagues certainly enjoy him. Also, Jim is excellent with him, very competent at feeding, bathing, changing and so on, which makes me relatively free after 4.00 p.m. I have also become rather involved in the activities of the Business and Professional Women's Club here. So you see I am not in much danger of turning into a vegetable just yet.

Jim and I continue to find life in Ndola very agreeable, despite petrol rationing and shortages of this and that due to the Rhodesian situation. Zambia has so organised things that this country is suffering far more from the results of economic sanctions against Ian Smith and his white government than Rhodesia itself. Previously most of our commodities came from Rhodesia, quickly and easily transported across the border. Now other more expensive sources of supply are being found. We are keeping our fingers crossed for Rhodesia. It would be wonderful if a solution to the problem could be found, but Messrs. Smith and Wilson hardly speak the same language. The Rhodesians regard Rhodesia as belonging to them in much the same way as England belongs to the English, or Greece to the Greeks, whereas outside powers regard it as belonging to the Africans. It would be nice to think that power could be shared, but in present-day Africa this is impossible. Our sympathies lie with the white Africans there, but I won't bore you with another long treatise on our pro-Rhodesian ideas. You possibly see the situation in quite a different light, as do most of our new expatriate friends. We should like to go to Salisbury for Christmas, but are a bit worried about possible thugery on the part of 'freedom fighters' en route. The journey involves several hundred miles of travelling over lonely roads, and the odd bullet makes its way through car windows just as a kind of gesture. We shall have to see what the position is in December. It may be more expedient to remain in peaceful Ndola.

You kindly asked what you can get for our infant son. What about a couple of those cover-all plastic bibs one can buy in England? Here it is only possible to get silly little ones that just fit round the neck, and young Laurence is already beginning to discover that fingers can be poked into food. Alternatively a Tommy Tippy baby cup or a special baby feeding dish would be useful. It is difficult to obtain these things in Zambia. I wonder whether we shall see you again next year? We should like to take a few weeks overseas leave but a lot depends on the state of our finances. After Jim qualifies for his African pension we are thinking of jumping on to the expatriate bandwaggon, so that the British taxpayer will make a large contribution towards the cost of our overseas lives. An expatriate officer is one who takes a contract offered by the British Government as part of its 'aid to underdeveloped countries.' In such cases a substantial part of the salary, and fares to Britain every year, or twice a year for those with school age children, the latter being accommodated at expensive boarding schools in England, also at British Government expense. One sometimes wonders how much the British public know about all this overseas aid. Our long home leave last year was paid for by the old Federal Government, for which Jim had worked since 1955. After that he became a permanent Zambian civil servant, which means we must take holidays at our own expense.

Now it is Laurence's play hour. Time with Mother. At the moment he is gurgling away in his playpen, a potentially useful piece of equipment into which he has been put right from the start. It is a big square wooden pen that now contains a blanket over the floor, a small mattress, and loads of toys. He sleeps or wakes as the mood takes him, and can see me, and most things that are going on in the flat through the slats and the open door. The idea of putting him in it so soon is the assumption that he will become accustomed to being there, and there should not be problems when he becomes more aware.

January 1967

Dear Ruth,

Thank you so very much for the splendid bibs you sent for Laurence. They are just what he needed. He already tries to feed himself, preferring fingers to spoons so you can imagine the mess that results. Fortunately we have organised a large, more or less child proof nursery for him, so we don't bother much about mess. Anyway, our very good servant Byson does the cleaning up. Laurence is becoming ever more lively. He can already crawl, and gets around like a bullet on his hands and knees. Jim has fixed a gate across the nursery doorway so that he can't escape into danger areas. Of course we also have our big square playpen and he has no objection to being placed inside it, together with a good selection of toys. This is particularly useful for tennis days. We pile it into the back of the car, and then set it up on the club lawn. This means Jim and I can go on to the courts at the same time without being overly concerned about the baby. He is used to it, and laughs his way through the afternoon, punctuated by drinks of ribena or orange juice, sponge biscuits, and the attention of players standing out. I am enclosing some up-to-date photographs for you. Isn't he a merry little fellow?

I hope you had a happy Christmas, not too cold. We joined our rebellious friends in Rhodesia for the festivities. I think I told you we were thinking of going to Salisbury, and indeed we did, and the only thugery we came across was the theft of some of Laurence's nappies and baby clothes from the washing line. Jim applied for a fortnight's local leave, but was only allowed four days, plus the bank holidays, so it was a bit rushed. However, it was good to see some well-stocked shops again, and to be able to get all the petrol we needed without difficulty. Salisbury appears to be booming. So far economic sanctions and British disapproval have had no obvious effect. There is a virtual absence of British goods in the shops, but plenty from other places, including France and West Germany, which seems rather surprising. The independence issue lingers on, doesn't it? The Rhodesian people are finding the uncertainty of the situation a little wearing, but they remain as determined as ever. If anything, views are becoming more entrenched and more extreme as time goes on. There is even talk of copying South Africa's apartheid system, and this is a new attitude in Rhodesia, probably arising from the fact that their survival is being threatened. What a pity an amicable agreement could

Laurence and Pam

Laurence – 7 months

Laurence – 7 months

Laurence – 7 months

not be reached! As time passes the chances of this happening are getting ever more remote.

Meanwhile, Jim and I are still enjoying life in Ndola, where there are plenty of satisfying activities. The Citizen's Advice Bureau that a group of us are trying to form has still not materialised. I wrote about our efforts last year. We have an office and a telephone. The difficulty now is getting enough African support. Without this, we might as well forget about the whole idea, since any predominantly European group is highly suspect in Zambia and would never get government permission to operate. We continue to hold weekly committee meetings, but, as is the case with most committees, there is a good deal more 'talk' than 'do'. However, we have contacted the local political leaders about it. They express interest, but will not actively participate. The next step will probably have to be a bit of leg work round the African townships to try to enlist support from their Residents' Associations.

I have also recently been asked if I will become secretary of the Marriage Guidance Society. I was under the impression that this organisation was more or less defunct. It stopped operating when Zambia became independent, but it now seems that somebody is trying to get it going again. I was approached about the matter in the middle of a Business and Professional Women's tea party in front of an army of women, so I wasn't really able to discus the proposal, but I have agreed to attend a meeting about it. At least the Marriage Guidance Society can claim to exist already, or it did in the past, so it will not have to get government permission, as all new organisations must do. Yet I don't want to take on too many responsibilities.

We are thinking about taking a month's overseas leave in June to introduce Laurence to the country where he belongs, and to meet his English relatives. We will try to get to see you while we are there, but much will depend on where we stay.

October

Dear Ruth,

We can fully sympathise with you over the price of property. We were in the UK for a few weeks in June / July, taking a very brief leave. With the future in mind we interested ourselves in housing etc., and were horrified at the amount of money we shall have to spend when we decide to settle down. Heaven Help Us! We haven't even any furniture of our own so will need an immediate sum of money for that. It was a pity we were not able to see you, but we were there for such a short time and it was impossible to fit everything in. It is not so easy to hop around the country with an infant in tow, even an amenable infant such as Laurence. Also I had a threatened miscarriage at the time, which added to our difficulties. However, we much enjoyed our leave. We rented a charming olde worlde cottage called Clare's Cottage in the Kentish village of Throwley Forstal, near Faversham. I found a nice doctor in Faversham who gave me injections to prevent the miscarriage, and advised me not to dash around too much. He suggested bed rest might be a good idea, but for me it was a thoroughly bad idea because it was impossible. With the cottage, included in the rent, was a lady who came every morning to keep it clean, and this was a bonus. We entertained as many people in Throwley as we could fit into the available time. Laurence celebrated his first birthday there, and on that day he began to walk. The uncharacteristic weather, warm and sunny for most of the time, gave us some affection for that part of the country, and we were really sorry when the time came to return to Ndola.

In my absence I had been elected Secretary of the Marriage Guidance Society of Ndola and the resulting correspondence, organisation of meetings, and so forth, involves me in several hours work each week. I was not best pleased about it because I wanted time to consider the proposition, but it seemed to be a fait accompli Next we must decide what to do to make it into a going concern again.

My pregnancy has survived, and Penelope Jane is due in early December. At least I hope it's Penelope Jane. I don't know that, and Jim says it won't be a girl because his brother has boys and his father had boys. But I, and all the neighbours, call 'it' Penelope Jane, in anticipation.

Laurence is now 16 months, and in one of the photos I enclose he is giving himself a clap because he has just put all the shapes in the correct holes in the post box Jim had to put a canvas cover round the balcony railings because he tried to climb through. He is too big, but he might just get his head jammed.

Next time I write he will have a sibling, hopefully a sister.

January 1968

Dear Ruth,

This is just a quickie to tell you that our daughter, Penelope Jane, was born on 7th December. Yes, she is here. Our small group of parents in Cecil Court were having a dinner party together at the time, and Jim was there, in between visits to the hospital, so they all shared in the delight. We had talked about Penelope Jane for so long, and now she is here. She weighed 6lb.11oz and was born with a surprising quantity of dark hair. She is thriving, and never gets us up in the middle of the night, for which we are truly thankful. When she was three weeks old I started to give her the nightly baby cereal by spoon instead of putting it in the bottle. The nurse at the baby clinic suggested

Laurence – 16 months

Laurence – 16 months

this. Rather an extreme form of early learning I thought, but Penelope doesn't care. She opens her mouth for it like a little bird. Feeding sessions come round with monotonous regularity. She has a hearty appetite, the same as Laurence, but at least I have specified times and we both understand what the routine is. There is a growing trend towards 'feeding on demand', like the Africans. Hmm. For me that is a definite "no no". She shares the nursery with Laurence, and sleeps in the cot, which is hand-made and has no slats and thus Laurence can't poke her. Laurence has been upgraded to a bed. He is fascinated by hs sister and shows few signs of jealousy, although he has become more demanding than he used to be. On the whole, though, he remains an exceptionally good-humoured child who will spend hours playing on his own in the nursery with his toys and books. He is a great chatterbox and talks very fluently for his age. He also now attends a mornings only Nursery Playgroup, which he calls school, and seems to thoroughly enjoy. He is not properly toilet trained, which is a condition of entry, but he knows what the potty is for and always uses it when I sit him there. I put him in a nappy at night, or when I am taking him out, otherwise it is not necessary and I see no point in washing more nappies than I have to. At the playgroup there is much the same system, so that both of the nappies I send with him come home dry.

We are soldiering on in Ndola amidst many difficulties and frustrations. Just now we are in the middle of another great petrol crisis. All the garages are dry, and we are more or les imprisoned in the flat, with two cars standing idle in the back yard. In a country where there is no public transport a car is a vital necessity. We have been promised five gallons per car for the month of February. This will be better than nothing, though most of us use a good deal more than that every week. We bought a new cortina station wagon in December to accommodate our increased family and it is frustrating not to be able to use it. Zambia has just gone over to a decimal system of currency. We now work in 'kwacha'

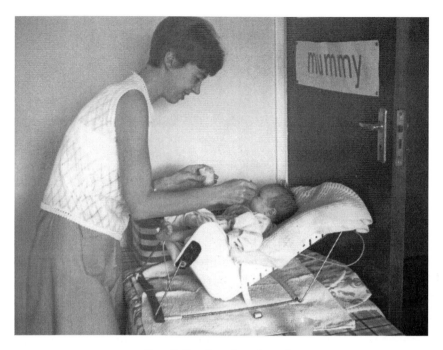

Pam & Penelope Jane 3 weeks

Jim & Penelope Jane 3 weeks

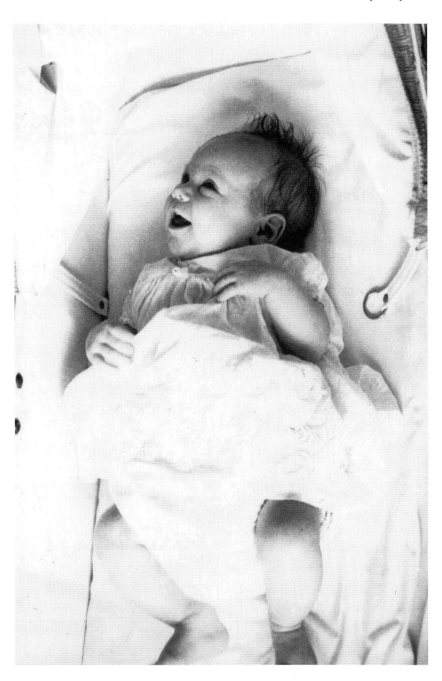

Penelope – 6 weeks

and 'ngwee' which at present seems strange and vaguely amusing. Doubtless we shall soon become accustomed to it.

Rhodesia appears to be weathering the storm, much to our delight. Petrol there flows freely, and the shops are packed with commodities unavailable in the black north. Our Rhodesian friends take great pleasure in sending various items to us because they have ceased to be obtainable here. Britain has plenty of economic problems of her own at the moment so perhaps she will not have time to worry too much about Rhodesia, but we continue to wonder how long it can last.

Jim's present contract finishes in 1969. We have not finally decided whether to make the break with Africa at that point. The thought of returning to the UK is not pleasing, but we shall have to do it sooner or later because the children will need to be educated. Needless to say, I would like to give Rhodesia a try but Jim, who is more sane and sensible, and more pessimistic, says this is not an option. We cannot turn them into little Rhodesians only to be thrown out, or worse, by the bellowing black majority. My words, not his. He simply said that it is not an option because of the unsettled political situation. In any case we shall be in England in the summer of 1969 and I very much hope we shall see you then.

It is time to feed Penelope Jane again. She is now six weeks old, and she is looking hopeful, waving her arm and smiling at me.

July

Dear Ruth,

Zambia is going through what is being called an 'economic revolution', which has created an atmosphere of confusion in the country. What it amounts to is a great speeding up of the Africanisation policy. The government has compulsorily acquired a majority of shares in all commercial enterprises. Henceforth non-Zambians are forbidden to own trading businesses or other small concerns, and can no longer borrow money from financial institutions or banks. All this was to be expected but it has led to another exodus of Europeans, and a general feeling of disquiet.

Meanwhile we carry on happily enough in Ndola. I am still doing a fair amount of voluntary social work. We managed to get the Marriage Guidance Society of Zambia up and running again. We decided to make pre-marriage counselling our main focus. Three of us, a psychologist, a fellow social worker, and I, are running group discussions on Growing Up with the school-leavers at the local secondary schools. This has turned out to be a very interesting experience. The young people are aged 16+ and come from a wide variety of racial and cultural backgrounds. We cover a number of issues, such as budgeting, basic child care, nutrition, conflict with parents, future careers, job interviews, sex, and, most important of all, relationships. The children all have lively minds and their own ideas, though most of them reflect the religious and cultural background in which they were brought up. But they are not afraid to have their views questioned by others and to talk about different ways of living. As you might imagine, the Western Europeans express the most independent thoughts. We ourselves are learning more than we teach. One little Asian girl is about to be married to her parents' choice of husband for her without knowing much about him. She expressed anxiety about the 'first night' but said she thought her parents were wise, and she trusted them, and went on to talk about what she has seen of western romantic marriage, and the number of times things go wrong with it. An African student said he thought their way was kinder than ours because, even though they might have more than one wife, they did not desert the first one but continued to care for her in the same village, and support her financially. We hope they are finding the sharing of views as valuable as we do. The only problem with setting up the groups was that some of the parents objected to it, thinking we might try to convert their children to our western ways. We therefore ran a couple of group sessions for parents to explain what we were doing and to invite those who had doubts to withdraw their children, since it was not compulsory. Nobody was withdrawn.

We also do a limited amount of marriage counselling. I hope this last remains limited since we are thin on the ground as far as personnel are concerned, and dealing with warring spouses is not my favourite social work task.

In addition to all this I am now Ndola's representative for the Child Care and Adoption Society of Zambia. This is the only registered Adoption Society in the country, but the work is not particularly arduous because there are so few adoptions taking place here these days. I do a good deal of visiting in connection with applications to adopt, but much less with unmarried mothers who wish to place their children for adoption. Hence there is a great shortage of babies and the waiting list is long. But it keeps my hand in.

I am also heavily involved in the activities of the Business and Professional Women's Club, and am on the committee. So you see I am well-occupied, babies notwithstanding. But I like to be active outside the home, and to have stimulating company. Wallowing in excess domesticity is disagreeable.

The children are flourishing, and they are both full of good humour. Laurence is two now, and likes to assert himself, but he is a reasonable little fellow and easy to handle. He has a large vocabulary and is for ever asking questions, and he loves the company of other children. Penelope Jane is happy and contented for most of the time. We thought Laurence was a good baby but she is straight from heaven. I often take her with me on my morning visits, as I did Laurence, but I also have plenty of friends who are happy to look after her. The enclosed photographs were taken on Laurence's second birthday.

Next month we are off to our beloved Rhodesia for a few days. It will be interesting to see what things are like there now. We have not been since Christmas 1966, but we gather that the Rhodesians are as full of hope as ever.

Life in the UK sounds most depressing and the prospect of returning there to live does not exactly fill us with joy. However, since there appears to be no future for us here in Africa we have no alternative, and the probable plan is to settle down somewhere in the south of England in 1969. Ugh! How we shall miss Zambia's constant sunshine. We are booked to sail from Durban on the east coast of South Africa on a ship called the SA Vaal in April next year. The Vaal is a classless ship so we won't have any first class passengers to envy. It's a long way round, but by this method we get a cruise around the South African coast, calling at the coastal towns, before we sail across the Atlantic. We shall bring with us one of the cars and as many of our goods and chattels as is practical, unless anything crops up to change our minds. Believe me, it would not take much of an alternative offer for me to change my mind.

Some Facts About Zambia

Zambia is an independent republic in central Africa and a member of the Commonwealth. It is entirely within the tropics and is more than three times the size of Britain. The Zambezi River rises in the northwest corner of Zambia and flows through the country to Livingstone dropping through a gorge about 120 metres deep to form the Victoria Falls. Farther down its course it enters Kariba Lake which was formed by damming the river in Kariba Gorge. The dam has supplied electric power to Zambia and Zimbabwe since 1960. The Zambezi makes its way through Mozambique heading

Laurence drawing – aged 2yrs

Laurence & Pam playing

Jim with Laurence and Penelope on blanket

Penelope and Laurence jumping in puddles after a tropical storm

towards the Indian Ocean. The area now called Zambia was first named after this river. It was called Zambezia. The river divides it from Zimbabwe. Other counties that surround it are Angola, Zaire, Tanzania, Malawi, Mozambique, Botswana and Namibia.

Early humans were said to have inhabited the area more than a million years ago. The first of the country's modern tribes, the Tonga, appear to have settled in the Zambezi Valley around 1500AD. They were followed by other Bantu tribes from the northwest. In the 1830s Bantu tribes from southern Africa also arrived and settled in the country. At roughly this time Arab slave traders from the north-west and Portuguese slave traders from Angola entered Zambia and for years they continued to carry off people as slaves.

David Livingstone was partly responsible for opening up this country to Europeans. He reached Zambia in the mid nineteenth century. He travelled up the Zambezi River in the 1850s hoping to introduce Christianity and European civilisation and to combat the misery of the Arab slave trade. He "discovered" the magnificent water falls on the border between Zambia and Zimbabwe in 1855, and he named them the Victoria Falls after Queen Victoria. Livingstone's efforts attracted other missionaries, who in turn brought hunters and prospectors in their wake. In the 1890s Cecil Rhodes (see Rhodesia) was pursuing his plans to expand the British Empire. When he arrived in Zambia he made treaties with most of the African chiefs as part of his plan to gain power over the territory. In 1911 he put it under the control of the company he had founded, the British South Africa Company, and the country became known as Northern Rhodesia. At about the same time vast copper ore deposits were found in the north-central part of the territory, the area now called the Copperbelt. Large-scale mining operations were set up around the town of Kitwe, and local Africans were employed as labourers.

This region was put under direct British control as a British Protectorate in 1924. By then more Europeans had started to move in and they gained considerable power in the country and were an asset in establishing economic progress. In 1953 Northern Rhodesia was made part of the Federation of Rhodesia and Nyasaland, much against the wishes of the natives because they thought it gave too much power to the Europeans. There was already a lobby group asking for African independence, and this movement now became stronger.

When the Federation was dissolved in December 1963 the African struggle for independence in Northern Rhodesia was nearly over. Kenneth Kaunda had become President of the United National Independence Party, and under his leadership the country became an independent African state on 24th October 1964 under the name of Zambia. Kaunda rapidly bankrupted the country. His government was wracked by corruption and mismanagement, and falling copper prices and rising fuel prices accelerated the slide into poverty. It used to be a middle-income state, but by the end of the 1970s Zambia was one of the world's poorest countries, and it still is.

Zambia is rich in mineral resources. Copper is the chief export. Lead and zinc are also exported, and some coal is mined. The 1999 slump in world copper prices was disastrous for Zambia's economy because copper forms 80% of Zambia's exports. Mining is a useful provider of employment. Agriculture is the major occupation. The main subsistence crop is maize, grown by virtually all Africans. From it they make the mealie meal porridge that forms their basic daily food. Cash crops include tobacco, groundnuts, cotton and sugar. Livestock and forestry are also important. There has been a huge decline in commercial farming over the course of the past forty-five years, and Zambia changed from a middle-of-the-road country to a poor one.

The population of Zambia is mostly African, largely Bantu, with minorities of Europeans, Asians and Chinese. Unemployment is high and many Africans live entirely on subsistence farming. Life expectancy is low, and AIDS is an on-going problem. The country depends on international aid in all its many forms. In April 2005 the World Bank approved a $3.8 billion debt relief package for the country. Many charitable aid agencies are busy there, and lots of volunteers with various skills do a spell in Zambia.

Europeans and other foreign settlers were not driven out of

Zambia after independence. A lot of them left because they wanted to, but some stayed on and there are a number of British tobacco farmers still working their highly successful farms on a commercial basis. I have an acquaintance who recently visited Zambia, with her husband, as guests of a relative who owns such a farm, and they were well impressed. The plantation is large and needs a big labour force and thus it provides employment for a considerable number of Africans. The visitors found themselves amongst a group of cheerful, well-fed people. Each family is provided with a small house, linked up to electricity, with a patch of garden in which to grow their maize and other vegetables. There is a primary school on site, and also a health clinic. It sounded similar to those days of long ago, when we lived there. The visitors were taken on a tour of parts of the country, to a game reserve and to the Victoria Falls. They could see the scantily clad children and adults trying to scrape a meagre living from the land. They came back home with a better understanding of the central Africa situation.

Zambia gained independence in 1964 when Kenneth Kaunda became president. His party was the United National Independence Party. In 1972 a new constitution led to one party rule and Kaunda reigned supreme until 1990. In that year there was mounting domestic pressure to oust Kaunda from power. Violent protests and an attempted coup led to the legalisation of opposition parties. Elections were held in 1991 and Kaunda was roundly defeated. After this Zambia became a multi-party democratic Republic with elections held every five years. There are some reports of corruption and rigged votes but Zambia has lots of natural resources to work with and, by and large, there is every reason for optimism about the country's continued development and future prosperity.

Six

An English Interlude 1969–1971

1969

Dear Ruth,

We did it. Sorrowfully, we left Ndola at the end of March and set off on the journey that would bring us to the UK. It was an extremely sad leave-taking with many tears and expressions of deep regret. So many friends who knew us well were upset by it, especially for me. Jim was less despondent, and more certain that this is what we must do. I was still not sure it was right, and the more I thought of England, and adjusting to life in a cold climate again, and the pattern of the working day, I became less sure than ever. Our servant Byson was upset too, even though there were still plenty of jobs around, and he had a brilliant reference from us. This is one of the last photos we took of our children at Cecil Court. There had just been a tropical storm and they were enjoying jumping in the puddles on the balcony. The box-like thing behind them is the lid of my old cabin trunk that I brought out on the Caernarvon Castle nearly a decade ago. What a flood has passed under the bridge since then.

Well, we piled into the car and set off on a journey through Rhodesia and South Africa visiting friends who had elected to remain in Africa along the way. I felt as if I were deserting a sinking ship, although the Rhodesian people still feel positive about their country's survival, and those in South Africa are sure of it. After a week of travelling we arrived in Durban and boarded the ship. The

This is Byson and his family, a faithful servant for 3 ½ years

Byson with Penny and Laurence

ship sailed on 7th April for a three week voyage to Southampton. We were used to the routine on a ship, but of course this was a first for the children, and they were fascinated by it. Each time we took them on deck they tried to climb on the railings to look at the sea throwing up white foam and speeding by. One went one way and the other in the opposite direction, and we had to watch them like hawks. Needless to say, they spent most of the day in the children's room, where they were entertained by a host of activities. They were well used to other children, and sharing play equipment, and singing action songs etc, and they willingly joined in with everything on offer. We took then on deck for a daily walk and to get some sea air, but were always filled with apprehension because they move so quickly, and the decks were always crowded with fellow passengers, and stewards delivering drinks and snacks. Most of our parenting tasks were done in the cabins. We had two cabins and a small collection of books and toys. The only problem we had on board was that people with children had to go to the first meal sitting whereas we much preferred the second. It was OK for lunch, though it didn't allow much time for pre-lunch drinks. But dinner was a bit chaotic. Children's supper was at 5.00 p.m. and this they ate with gusto. But then we had to bath them and get them to bed in time for our dinner, which began at 6.30. They were not always asleep by then so we were often late getting to the dining room, and dinner had to be rushed so that the staff could get us finished and prepare for the second sitting. Not the best possible arrangement. The ship stopped for a while at the ports of East London, Port Elizabeth, and Cape Town and each time we were able to go ashore, and we saw, and said goodbye, to our friends in Port Elizabeth and in Cape Town. The enclosed photograph was taken while we were anchored in Cape Town and you can see Table Mountain in the background. The South Africans slobber with affection over this mountain. They seem to see it as a national symbol, and one has to admit it is quite impressive.

We duly arrived at Southampton dock at the end of April. Our Ford Station Wagon had travelled on the ship with us and we

Penny and Laurence on Ship at Capetown.

piled into it and proceeded to the accommodation we were to rent for the next six months. This was the West Wing of a large house called Tiptoe Lodge and it was an idyllic place to stay. We had full use of the grounds with lawns, bushes, and trees for the children to play amongst, and there was even a swing. Tiptoe is just a hamlet with nothing there except the Hampshire countryside, but it is near to New Milton and the New Forest, and the wonderful summer made it possible to take picnics in the Forest, admire the ponies, and generally to have an agreeable few months. We bought a twin pushchair in which to secure the children when necessary. Very soon I got a temporary job based at my old university, Southampton. It was to take part in a survey of mentally handicapped children and their parents, under a psychiatrist called Dr Kushlick. We had to interview the families, collect a great deal of information about them, and analyse the results. Each interview was recorded on a tape recorder so that our own performance could be monitored. When Jim found work Dr Kushlick arranged for his neighbour to care for our children so that I could continue with the job, and the arrangement worked well. I was really sorry when I had to move on shortly before the completion of the project. Amidst all this I watched enthralled the landing on the moon of Neil Armstrong and Edwin Alden, the Apollo astronauts. Did you?

Clearly, the most important thing to do after we arrived in England was for Jim to find employment, and the second most important was to buy a house. Both these things have now been accomplished. Jim bought a second hand Morris Minor, since I needed our car, and initially he went to board with Edna and Arthur, old foster parents I had used when I worked for Middlesex County Council in the 1950s. They live in Potters Bar. To cut a long story short, he is now working for Eastern Electricity in Old Southgate, and we have bought a very nice four-bedroomed house in Hertford. Initially the house was not equipped with central heating and so the children and I moved into The White Horse Inn in Hertford while this most vital utility was installed. It did not take long, and we moved into the house in November. Thus we now have a house and a mortgage and we have begun our new and very different life as an English family. Here we are celebrating our first Christmas Day at 36 Ware Road, Hertford. We call the house Nyasa as a reminder of other times, and places where I would prefer to be.

Hertford July 1970

Dear Ruth,

We have now come to the end of our first working six months in Britain. You asked me how we are getting on. Well, what a culture shock it has been, and we, especially I, do not like it. First, I do not like the appalling climate. It's not a climate really, it's just weather, and it's totally unpredictable from one day to the next so one never knows what to wear, or how much protective clothing the children will need for the day. Second, I do not like the busy busy busy daily routine. Third, I do not like the necessary budgeting, and the tussle to earn enough money to live as comfortably as we wish, and to buy trivialities. I miss Africa, with its hot weather and lots of sunshine, and its easy lifestyle, even more than I thought I would.

Nevertheless I soon found a job that suits me. I am now a social worker for the NSPCC, covering Harlow Town and the surrounding area. I do twenty hours or so a week. My salary covers twenty, and if the job requires me to work more I claim for the extra hours. Occasionally I have to attend seminars that last all day, or go to London for a general staff meeting. But the big advantage of this job is that, by and large, I can do the hours at any time I like, including weekends, and this makes it easier to look after the children as well. I have two registered child minders to care for Penelope, so that they can cover for one another if there

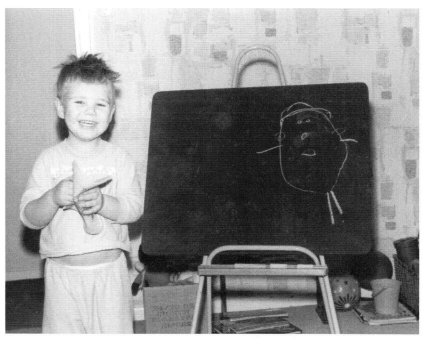

*25th December 1969. Laurence has just drawn on his new blackboard
a picture of a man that looks like a potato with legs.*

Pam with Children under Christmas tree

are problems. Laurence goes to a Playschool each morning in a village called Stanstead Abbotts. The daily routine is punishing compared with the more relaxed way of living to which we were accustomed. Jim leaves before 8.00 a.m. to catch the train to London, and he seldom gets home before 8.00 p.m., just in time for dinner. At around 8.30 in the morning I set off with the children. I take Penelope either to Ware, to a very nice Irish lady with five children, including two lots of twins, or to my friend Mary who has one little boy. Then I take Laurence to the playschool, and proceed to Harlow, where I have an office, a telephone, a filing cabinet, and records of a collection of families with problems, and these have to be supervised. I collect Laurence at around 12.30 and Penelope in the early afternoon. Most afternoons we potter around at home. If the weather is good enough the children play in the garden, where we have provided plenty of play equipment including a climbing frame, a see-saw, a wendy house, a paddling pool, tricycles and push along toys.

There is a conservatory attached to our house, with doors opening on to the patio, and this conservatory is used as a playroom. We usually have a session with books at some stage, and they frequently play with the neighbour's children. Occasionally I take them to the park, where I meet other mothers doing the same thing, and this is intensely boring. I do a bit of housework, prepare meals, and at six o'clock, fortified by gins and tonic, I bath the children and get them ready for bed. There is often a minor skirmish over whose turn it is to sit at the tap end, unpopular because it gets in the way of bath toy play. Later Jim and I have a civilised dinner. Not exactly an exciting life, is it?

However, a little exciting news came from Rhodesia. As you probably know, on 2nd March Ian Smith declared that his country is now a republic, thus breaking Rhodesia's

July 1970; Garden Play

80-year-old links with Britain and effectively blocking the British government's efforts to steer its former colony towards black majority rule. No need to say that the new status is not generally recognised in the international community.

December 1970

Dear Ruth,

Christmas time, and this is just a short note to send you seasonal greetings and all good wishes for the New Year. I expect you got our card, but I had no time to write just then. We celebrated Christmas in the usual British way, with large quantities of traditional food and opening presents beside a Christmas tree, with a photograph to remember it by.

The new school year began in September of course, and since Laurence is now 4 we found a place for him at an independent school called Sherrardswood, near Welwyn. This school has very small classes and a good old fashioned infant teacher called Mrs Jamieson taking the reception class. It means that he will learn to read and write by the phonetics method and I shall be able to help him along the way. I do not favour the more fashionable 'look and say' system, which is illogical, and depends entirely on memory, good or bad. The school day at this stage is from nine until three and thus I have had to organise my time differently. Penelope has to stay with her child minder until after I have picked up Laurence, so nowadays I cram as many work hours as possible into four days a week and do the rest at weekends so that I can spend one day a week with Penelope. Jim does a lot of the child care over the weekend anyway, although, weather permitting, we try to take them on a special outing on either Saturday or Sunday, such as a visit to Whipsnade or some historic house or garden or to a museum in a nearby town or for a picnic in the country. We have had a few lovely weekends when we were able to do this, but I see no joy in walking around a zoo, or whatever, in the pouring rain. Sherrardswood School requires the children to wear school uniform and therefore we needed to buy Laurence a lot of new clothes. I enclose a photograph of him dressed for a school day in his purple blazer and cap, and grey shorts and socks. The school badge is a triangle with a growing tree inside it. The photo was taken in August, and he was not used to formal clothing, but he looks quite smart doesn't he?

Apart from this, there has been no great change in our lives since I wrote in the summer. Hertford is a nice little town and the people friendly. We are members of a baby-sitting group which enables us to have a night out sometimes, but there are not many places to go. There is no theatre, and even though we are not far from the bright lights of London it is too far to get there and back in an evening, and the children are still too young to appreciate the London scene. Thus the year 1970 has been one of plodding along trying to be English. The funny thing is that when we were overseas I felt very English indeed, but now we are here I feel like a foreigner in my own country. It should have been a year of adjustment but, at least on my part, no adjustment has taken place. The children, though, have shown remarkable resilience and have come smiling through.

July 1971

Dear Ruth,

Now what is in the melting pot? You may well ask, because there have been new developments since Christmas and my negative mood has changed to one of hope and optimism. The end of our time as a typical prudential family is coming soon because we are now expecting our third child. We decided on 'now' mostly because I am 36 and didn't want to get so old that it was no longer possible. I need not have worried

Laurence in School Uniform

about that because it happened without delay, the same as it did earlier. Also, on my part, I wanted to be young enough to bring up three children and still have enough energy to spare for a stimulating life of my own. Hertford is not in the least stimulating of course.

We know there can be more to life than a nice house and garden and English country parks and we have been talking of changing it for some place more interesting. We have looked at job advertisements in the national press and see that there are openings overseas with certain companies for people with Jim's skills. I can almost hear you gasp at the outlandish idea of going off to foreign parts with three small children in tow because the general feeling around here is that we must be mad. But that is what I would like to do, and I intend to take whatever steps I can to make it happen. As for the children, remember that two of them have already had the experience of being two blonde Zambians, as the Africans jokingly called them, and the third one will be too young to have an opinion. It would surely enrich their lives so, once again, watch this space. At least it gives me something to hope for even if it never comes to pass.

November 1971

Our son, Jeremy Rupert, was born on 3rd September. I wanted to call him Rupert but Jim said this would put him in danger of being called Pooh. I didn't send out a load of cards announcing his arrival because nobody was going to get overly excited about a third child, and Christmas is not far away which means one card can do for both. The baby was born at home, despite my age and my Rhesus Negative blood group, since home births are fashionable hereabouts. He was HUGE, weighing in at 9lb.12oz He was born with a mass of red curly hair, similar to Jim's when he was younger. If you recall, the September weather was unusually fine and warm and we were able to take him out into the garden when he was only a few days old. I enclose copies of the photographs we took at that time. He was already smiling at me, and don't tell me it was just wind because I know it was not. The photographs I have enclosed were taken when he was just 4 days old. Penelope and Laurence wanted to be included in my letter, so I have included one of them on their trikes in the garden. Penelope Jane is very jealous of the baby because, she said, 'I wanted to be the youngest'.

Shortly after this came a period of angst because our new son started to vomit back all his food. It turned out that he had pyloric stenosis, and at the age of 17 days he went into Queen Elizabeth Hospital in Welwyn Garden City for an operation to cure the condition. The young surgeon who did the operation accidentally nicked the mucosa and therefore wee Jeremy had to be drip-fed for five days until it had healed. He lost 3 lbs. in weight and came out of hospital weighing only 6lb. 8oz., so it was fortunate that he was such a whopper to begin with.

Jeremy's arrival was the big event of the year, but a close second is the fact that Jim has been offered a job overseas with a company called International Aeradio Ltd. He accepted the job and it is being arranged for him to go out next month, just after Christmas, and the children and I will follow in the New Year. Believe it or not, we have been posted to Lusaka, so back we go to Zambia. Hurrah! Zambia has had black government rule for seven years, and we wonder how life will be now. Clearly they still need to recruit British staff to keep things running.

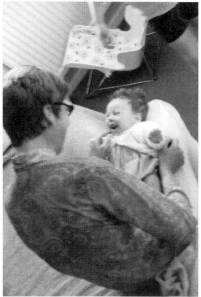

Jim & Jeremy age 4 days   *Pam & Jeremy age 4 days*

Posing for their turn

Seven

Back In Zambia 1971–1974

July 1972

Dear Ruth,

It all happened as planned. Jim came to Lusaka in December 1971, and I followed with the children in February 1972. It took a while to settle down here. As you and other friends had predicted, travelling across the world with three very young children is a different ball game from going as a free spirit, unencumbered by responsibilities for other people's lives. To go back to the beginning, the flight from Heathrow to Lusaka was long (15 hours) and fraught. Laurence and Penelope were extremely excited and, despite having been fed and washed and put in pyjamas at Heathrow, they did not settle down to sleep in the usual way. They ate most of my dinner between them and then got out their books and pencils and played about while most people were trying to sleep. They didn't make a noise, but Penelope kept wanting to go to the loo because she found it fun to walk up and down the plane. Eventually she caused a disturbance and gave herself a fright by locking herself in the lavatory. Jeremy behaved impeccably and fellow passengers expressed astonishment at how good he was, which partly made up for his siblings' restlessness. He slept soundly all night in the carry cot provided for him by the crew and I had to wake him in the morning to feed and change him. We landed at Lusaka Airport mid morning and I staggered off the aircraft with Jeremy in a carrying chair on my back, and trying to hang on to an energetic child on each side, and the hand luggage of clothes, nappies, and toys. Jim was waiting there for us and all three children went berserk with pleasure because, as they saw it, 'my daddy has come back'. Even little Jeremy, aged 5 months, bounced up and down and stretched out his arms in delight. We were taken to Lusaka Hotel in the middle of town, which was an unsuitable setting to be in with children. We had two rooms there, and the one in which Jim and I slept smelt of dog because Jim and been sharing it with a friend who brought his hound out with him from UK We gave the children the odour-free room, but we soon complained about unsuitable family accommodation and we were moved a couple of miles out of town to Andrew's Motel, which was perfect. There was a spacious garden and a swimming pool, and all our meals were provided. Andrew and his wife are Greek and their Mediterranean food is delicious. We were in the motel for four months, but it was expensive for the company and in June we were allocated a house, while our childless colleagues were allowed to enjoy motel life for longer. The house is in Mpulungu Road, where several other IAL families are living.

Now I have a woman servant called Joyce, recommended by an expat. who was leaving Zambia, and she is excellent. Her duties are to keep the house clean, do the washing and ironing, and help look after the children. I do the cooking which is not so easy these days because there is such a shortage of commodities. Last time I tried to shop there were only toilet rolls, tins of baked beans, and a few basic groceries on offer. This shortage is caused by western sanctions against Rhodesia, and the Zambian Government's decision to import everything from less efficient sources of supply elsewhere, instead of getting them popped over the border at Livingstone. Rhodesia is still managing well, using South Africa as a lifeline, but we have not yet been able to visit our Rhodesian friends partly because such visits are frowned upon by Zambian politicians.

The children at Andrew's Motel

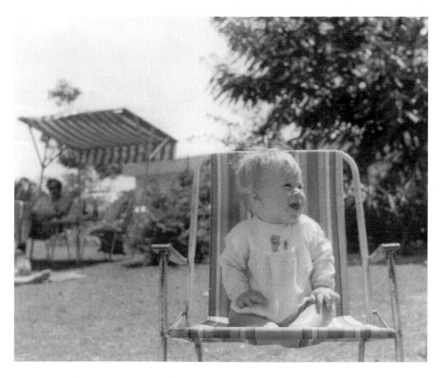

Jeremy at Andrew's Motel

Right from the start Laurence and Penelope entered into their new daily routine. Before we arrived here my friend Anne, who lives in Lusaka and has two children of similar age, had arranged for Laurence to attend the International School, and for Penelope to go to a playgroup to which her own daughter also goes. Penelope joined Laurence at the International School after Easter. Jim, while he was here on his own, had bought a car, a Renault 4, a very useful little car that has a strange gear system. The gear change lever is on the steering column, and this seems very odd. We only have one car and so I do a lot of running around, getting Jim to and from work, and the children to and from school, and then to their afternoon activities. Jim works shifts in a building some way out of town so sometimes it takes complicated organisation. The children have a very full and busy life, much richer than we were able to provide in UK. They get to school at around 7.45 a.m. ready to begin lessons at 8. The school morning lasts until 1.00 p.m., and the time is spent mostly on the academic stuff. It's a long morning, and they need sustenance during the mid morning break. Because of the shortage of goodies in the shops I have to bake cakes and biscuits and savouries to pack in their little 'lunch boxes'. I collect them at one and give them a cooked meal to keep them going for the afternoon. Also, they always have a bit of homework to do. Afternoon school is optional, and consists of activities such as Art, Craft, Games, Dancing, Acting, and such like things. They are expected to join one or two of these groups, and if they don't like, or get tired of, one thing they can change it for another. I take them back to school on three afternoons a week. The other two afternoons are devoted to swimming lessons at Lusaka public swimming pool, and both of them can now swim. Jeremy spends a lot of time with Joyce and her baby son Douglas. Two of his very first words were 'Doyce' and 'Douga', and he is happy and contented. Joyce lives in a little house at the bottom of the garden, but spends most of her time in mine, sometimes even all night if I have to take and fetch Jim for the night shift. I enclose a picture of Penelope doing one of her afternoon activities. I taught her to read myself shortly before she started school. She loves words and was a gratifyingly quick learner. I also enclose a photo of the children just back from school.

You asked if I am going to get a job. No, not at the moment. It's not a realistic possibility because old colonial types are none too welcome in the present Department of Social Welfare, and in any case I hop around so much it would be difficult to manage a working day. However, I am again involved in the work of the Child Care and Adoption Society of Zambia. The Society has recently built a Nutrition Rehabilitation Village which was officially opened last May. It takes in mothers with children under five who have just been discharged from hospital after treatment for malnutrition, usually either marasmus (starvation) or kwashiorkor (protein deficiency). It employs a number of staff to teach nutrition, cooking, home craft, gardening, cleaning, laundering, mending, knitting, sewing and suchlike skills, and it uses the basic food that the Africans eat in the villages, i.e. mealy meal, kapenta (dried fish), groundnuts, beans, milk, vegetables and fruit. Occasionally eggs for those who will eat them but some folk think eggs have an adverse effect on fertility, and it is very important to them to have children. It is their system of social care for later life, when the children will work and support the older people. I take a turn at bringing basic supplies into the village, offer words of encouragement and praise, and try to publicise the centre since the Society depends to a large extent on gifts and donations. An African social worker is employed to do follow-up family visits until the children reach the age of 5. I do my bit on certain mornings, and Jeremy is happy to stay with Joyce, but as I am the family chauffeur it depends who needs taking where.

Penelope and Laurence ready for school

The Nutrition Rehabilitation Village

Notes from The Child Care and Adoption Society - Zambia

The Nutrition Rehabilitation Village pamphlet cover

We have joined the Lusaka Central Sports Club, which has a swimming pool and tennis courts, but our use of this is relatively infrequent. We always seem to be doing something else during weekends, and sometimes Jim has to work.

Before I stop I must tell you about one other battle I fought. The International School is a fee-paying school and to begin with we had to pay the fees ourselves. Not cheap. Jim's conditions of work are supposed to include free education for the children, but IAL argued that there are free local schools available. There are, but all of them are full of black students, older than our children, whose first language is not English, and such schools are ill-suited to meet the needs of British pupils. Yet none of the other parents involved would support me. I asked one of them if she were not worried about her eight-year-old son, who can neither read nor write. She replied that she is not because she doesn't have clever children! My only ally was the headmaster of the local school I was supposed to use. He is British. I asked him what would happen if I sent my two very young and inquisitive children to his school. He raised his hands in horror and said the school was definitely unsuitable. He told me he sent his own children to the International School, said good things about it, and recommended that I do the same. 'Do you feel strongly enough to put that in writing?' I asked, and explained why it was necessary. Yes, he was more than willing to do this, and then I knew the battle was won. Very soon the company agreed to pay our school fees. You will not be surprised when I tell you that every single one of the parents who had met my concerns with disparagement immediately jumped on the bandwagon and now send their children to the International School. You need a car in order to get there. Some of the wives don't drive, and when husbands are on an unhelpful shift, guess what? I am roped in to take their children to school, along with mine. Hey Ho.

I am makeing a crocodile
WIth ELOY.

Age 4½

Penelope at a school art group.

December 1973

Dear Ruth,

It has been some time since I last wrote and this is because nothing in our lives has changed very much during the couple of years we have been back here. During the latter months of 1972 my friend Geraldine had a sabbatical from her job as head of a sixth form college and she decided to spend it exploring parts of Africa. She came to us in early August of that year bringing with her Alexander, her eight-year-old son, who is by no means an easy child. I think this is chiefly because of his somewhat stressful life caused by the acrimonious relationship of his divorced parents. I won't go into the details of how difficult he can be. However, we all went off to Kariba Dam for a short holiday, and that passed without too many incidents, although Geraldine was terrified of boating on the lake, which we did anyway, despite the fuss. I felt I had more cause for concern, since wee Jeremy, aged 11 months, was already walking and running about, but we were very careful, and it was Geraldine who wanted to go and see the dam, which we had already seen several times. There were no accidents in the water, but Alexander fell down a gravel slope and we had a big to-do over his grazed chin.

We returned to Lusaka without mishap, and then Geraldine went off on her travels again, leaving Alexander with us, and with instructions to put him on a flight to London in time for the beginning of term at The Dragon School. I was not best pleased, but somebody had to look after the poor child. He was mischievous, and I was afraid he would be a bad influence on my own well-behaved son and daughter. I need not have worried. They were very kind to him but they never tried to copy him, and during the few weeks he was with us there was a remarkable improvement in his behaviour. We had a drama however over getting him back home. Geraldine and Ian were having a row over who should meet him, and Lusaka airport staff would not

Jeremy – 11 months – at Keriba

At Kariba. Note Alexander's poorly chin, and the truculent look.

put him on his flight until they had the name and details of the person to whom they would hand him over in London. Thus he missed his flight and we had to book him on another one. I was not amused, but Alexander remained calm.

'Don't worry Pam', he said, 'One of them will be there'.

1972 ended with the usual celebration of Christmas, for which we joined forces with another family. Even Christmas is easier to manage, and more fun, in a hot country where one can be inside or outside without special clothing. Another Christmas now approaches. Jeremy has set his heart on getting a wheelbarrow, which raised the question of how could we find one. Amazingly, we found one, a toy wheelbarrow in red plastic just the right size for Jeremy, who is only two and very small for his age. Thus he will get his wish. He started a playgroup in September. He gets on well there, and enjoys being with other small children and playing with such a large assortment of play equipment, but he is always very pleased when I arrive to bring him home. Laurence and Penelope are making steady progress at the International School.

Soon after we had settled down here we came across an irritating local tax problem. Because we had previously been in Zambia for seven years, and two of our children were born here, we could not convince government officials we are now back on temporary contract from a British company, and therefore should be no more subject to tax than others employed by our company. They view us as local Zambians and see our two years in UK as no more than an extra long overseas leave, and we have to pay up. For this reason it is probable we shall get another posting next year. Well, it might be nice to go somewhere new.

Earlier this year a law was passed making it illegal for anybody to cross the border into Rhodesia, and this is a real downer for

us. *We have always looked forward to visiting Rhodesia to see
our friends and to find out how the land lies now. As time goes
by our misgivings are growing. There is escalating guerrilla
activity over there, operating from neighbouring Mozambique,
with frequent murders and terrorist attacks. Ian Smith has
lengthened the period of compulsory military service, and he
sanctions reprisals against any Africans suspected of helping
the guerrillas. To us this sounds like very bad news, but we are
told the stoical white population still has a positive attitude and
remains convinced that eventually it will win. It is impossible
for them to envisage that anyone would want to destroy such
a fantastic country, with a great national spirit, responsible
management, and, generally speaking, good race relations
and probably the most prosperous black people in Africa. We
fervently hope they are right, and good sense will l prevail, but
I have a dreadful feeling of foreboding.*

*Here in Zambia life is peaceful and agreeable, and for that
we are truly thankful. I enclose another snapshot of our three
cheerful children in the garden, enjoying their lives in the
sun.*

46 Mpulungu Road July 1973

Eight

All Change 1974–1975

December 1974

Dear Ruth,

We are now in Libya. Jim received notice of this posting at the end of last year and we left Lusaka in the spring of this year. In some ways it was another sad parting because who knows when, or if, we shall return to central Africa, which, in so many ways, feels like home?

In January I took Laurence and Penelope to Livingstone by coach so that they could see the Victoria Falls on the Zambezi River, which is one of the most spectacular sights in the world. Laurence was 7 1/2 and Penelope 6, and we thought they might be just old enough to remember it in years to come. Zambia is turning into a less efficient country than it used to be, and I was not surprised when one of the tyres on the coach had a puncture, and there was no spare wheel. Thus we were stranded on the side of the road for an hour or two while help was summoned. However, we eventually arrived at a very comfortable hotel in Livingstone, where we were entertained by attention-grabbing African dancers, and the children viewed the thundering Victoria Falls from several angles. A short distance along the road was the entry to Rhodesia, and it was tantalising for me not to be able to cross over into this amazing country. In the past it was always so easy. However, I did what I had set out to do, and I enclose a photo of the children beside the falls, and African men dancing a village dance. Maybe they will chalk it up to experience, and maybe they won't.

When we left Zambia we went back to our house in Hertford, and shortly afterwards we took Jim to Heathrow and saw him off to Tripoli, Libya. I was to pack and follow at a later date, and thus the children and I spent the summer in Hertford. There was just one term to go before the end of the school year so I sent Laurence and Penelope to the local primary school, which was nearby, and Jeremy stayed at home. Laurence was happy enough, but his education seemed to be on hold. However, he managed to pass the entrance exam to the prep department of Kimbolton School, ready for entrance this year. I had a problem with Penelope because of her reading prowess. The infant teacher gave reading lessons by showing pictures and asking the children to read the words underneath. Penelope was irate, and came home with a tale of total woe. Usually I try not to interfere with a teacher's methods in case it affects her relationship with my child, but it was impossible to let this go. I made a small collection of books that Penelope enjoyed reading, e.g. The Elves and the Shoemaker and Puss in Boots, and went to see her teacher, who was astonished. The result was she was put into a junior class for reading, and calm returned. It was a reasonable summer and Jeremy was happy to play in the garden with his trike, climbing frame, little house, and so on until the end of term, when the others were on holiday.

In August my friend Geraldine came with Alexander and we went on excursions to zoos, farms, gardens and houses open to the public, and interesting old towns. Geraldine helped me to sew labels on Laurence's school uniform and other clothes. Every handkerchief, shirt, sock, piece of sportswear, towel and so forth had to have a name tape stitched into the back, and it was a very tedious task. We also spent a few days with my mother in Gloucestershire, which was quite a long drive with three restless children strapped side by side on the back seat.

At the Victoria Falls, Zambia

At the Victoria Falls, Zambia

Jeremy on his Trike

In mid September Laurence started Kimbolton School. I left him there with some apprehension because the head of the Prep Department seems very authoritarian and strict. Laurence has always been disciplined at home, and he knows where the boundaries are, but he is used to a more informal approach, and he probably won't like the character-building regime of a boys' boarding school. But I hope we shall get what we are paying for, which is a well-rounded and good education, to include facilities for a number of different sports and an introduction to music and the arts, things that we cannot provide because of our own limiting background, Who knows whether this will work out in the long run?

After I had taken Laurence to school I went to join Jim in Tripoli with the other two children. Libya has been a republic since 1969 when Colonel Moamaar al Gadafi deposed King Idris in a coup. Gadafi is a martinet and he introduced a cultural revolution on strictly Islamic principles. This turns it into a difficult posting for western Europeans, and our kitchens are always full of buckets and bowls fermenting illegal alcoholic beverages. I am told that alcohol is available at vast cost on the black market, but I don't know how to access it even if we could afford it. The shops are not exactly full of goodies, but the local bakery produces good bread and there is a greengrocer who brings his van full of fresh vegetables and fruit to the house each week. We have a large but dilapidated house in Giorgimpopoli, a nice suburb of the city, with good beaches. My American neighbour and I can have conversations through a large crack in the veranda wall. There are several American oil companies here managing the oil wells, and they speak longingly of how much better things were when the Italians were in charge Well, yes, there are better places than this has become, and I much preferred life in Lusaka. Nevertheless Libya is an interesting country, and the ruins of the ancient Roman cities of Sabratha and Leptis Magna are absolutely fascinating.

We are making the most of what there is here. I acquired a free copy of the Quran from the large city mosque, one of many, and I and have dipped into it. It is a huge book of nearly 2,000 pages, and it includes an English translation and commentary I have also joined a small class of people learning Arabic, taught by a very amenable Palestinian gentleman. Despite the strong Muslim flavour of this country women are allowed to drive, and I have a car. I need it to chauffeur the children around. On the streets the military are everywhere, soldiers with guns. If Jim and I go out at night we can be stopped by one of them wanting to make sure I am his legal wife. There are always soldiers standing beside the British school, which Penelope attends. Jeremy, now aged three, goes to a nursery school run by the wife of one of Jim's colleagues. Outside the British School I met a young woman who has started a brownie pack. She described herself as Brown Owl, and asked if Penelope would like to join. I let slip the fact that once, long ago, I was myself a brownie. Silly me. The immediate response was to invite me to be Tawney Owl. Believe it or not, I went along with this. I thought it would be an outside interest for Penelope, because the school provides only basic education, mornings only. Thus Penelope and I are going to Brownies one evening a week, although neither of us much enjoy this activity. Penelope is not a groupie, and she can happily entertain herself with no trouble at all. Another activity the poor child has been dragged into is Sunday School, organised by Margaret, another wife of one of Jim's colleagues, who thinks her religious education is being neglected, and so it is. Now she spends Sunday afternoons singing little choruses and hymns, listening to bible stories, and drawing pictures. She seems not to mind too much, and it will be useful to her later on when she goes to an English boarding school in which Christian teaching will definitely be on the menu.

We have also joined a declining club called the Underwater Club, but there is not much there, just a little bar that sells coffee and soft drinks, a small swimming pool, a tennis court

Leptis Magna, Libya

Leptis Magna, Libya

Leptis Magna, Libya

Leptis Magna, Libya

and a nice beach. However, there I found somebody with whom to play tennis, a lady who was once in Nyasaland. I used to play tennis with her mother when she was a girl, away at school for much of the time. Now she is a woman with two little girls of her own.

At the end of the summer term the children all came home with their first school photographs, even wee Jeremy. I shall enclose some copies. You will notice that Penelope has lost her front teeth. She lost them a little on the early side due to a fall she had while staying with my mother.

Meanwhile we have been keeping our eyes on the situation in central Africa, and there is no comforting news from there. Zambia seems to be sinking into poverty and corruption, at least partly due to government mismanagement. The Rhodesians are still hanging on in there, but anxiety about the future is beginning to grow. We wonder what the next few years will bring. I hope, among other things, a more relaxed posting for Jim.

November 1975

Dear Ruth,

We have lived through another year coping with life in Libya as best we can, and it hasn't been too bad. The place has not changed since I wrote last year. We get pleasure from the sun and the beaches, and we enjoyed a trip into the mountains for a change of scenery, and another into the Sahara Desert where we collected some desert roses, which are made of crystallised sand. They are hard, and pinky brown in colour, and some of them look similar to a rose.

It is now winter, an unpleasantly chilly season even here, and I am writing this snuggled beside the space heater. This is a

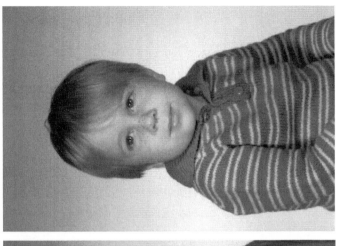

Jeremy

Penelope

46 Mpulungu Road July 1973

Laurence

large piece of equipment that stands in the central hall of the house. It drinks paraffin, and it is very effective.

We went on leave to England in June, and we spent much time looking for a school for Penelope. Kimbolton School had told us they were planning to take girls in their next entry and of course we put her name down for this, and Jeremy is down to go there in 1980. But now the school has changed its mind about having girl boarders. So much for sending the children all to the same school. Geraldine, who is a very experienced teacher, advised us to send her to an all-girls school because, she told us, girls tend to do better academically in a single sex school. We had been thinking in terms of co-education, and we looked into both, and then looked seriously at a few Girls Only schools. Frankly, there was not a great deal to choose between them. None of the schools were perfect, but what school is? In the end we went for the convenience of a school geographically near to Kimbolton to avoid long journeys in different directions. We chose Westwood House in Peterborough, and we have recently bought a house not too far from there, in a village called Sawtry, roughly half way between Cambridge and Peterborough. We had planned to keep Penelope at home for another year, when she would have been approaching 9, but we have heard that we are to get a new posting next year, and we have no idea what that might be like, so we decided to let her go this year. Westwood House is a school that takes children from prep school to sixth form, as does Kimbolton, and we trust this will bring some consistency into their lives. Their nomadic home life is full of ever-changing experience, giving them interesting contact with other lifestyles, other cultures, other races, different traditions, and, up to a point, different climates (we are not about to take them to the Antarctic). These things must surely be enriching, but one cannot pretend they make for stability.

We were in England for the end-of-year activities at Kimbolton, attending events such as parents' day, the school swimming gala, and a prep school concert. We met some very talented

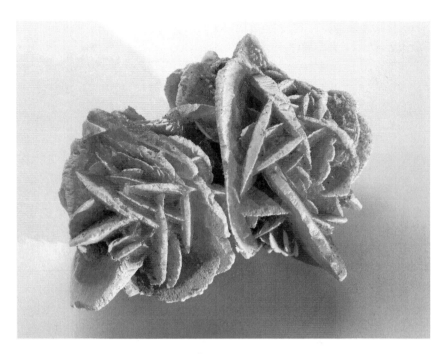

Desert rose

The trio on the beach at the Underwater Club

junior school teachers that more than make up for the head's rather strict methods of control. But we learned, to our dismay, that our Laurence is their 'Larry'. I asked the maths master where we would find Laurence. He looked greatly puzzled, and repeated my question.

'Yes', said I, 'our son, Laurence Cotton'. Enlightenment dawned.

'Ohhh. You mean our Larry'.

Indeed, Larry he had become.

The term ended early in July, and we went back to Libya with the three of them. They had a very long summer holiday covering July/August/September, and it is more difficult here to find things to do with them. They didn't much like trailing round old Roman cities with a guide book while I pontificated about the function of each building, especially in the summer heat. They preferred to be on the beach, and we made a lot of use of the unpretentious Underwater Club about which I told you.

As always, we are watching the central Africa situation, wondering whether we might ever go back, but there is nothing good about the news from there. Zambia is sinking from a moderately rich country into a very poor one. The collapse of world copper prices this year had a devastating effect on the economy, and they have no ideas on what to do about the situation. They could develop other sources of revenue, through agriculture, or even tourism, but the Africans are not given to lateral thinking.

The Rhodesians battle on, but their up-beat, positive approach is beginning to dwindle. This year two African militants, Joshua Nkomo and Robert Mugabe, joined forces to form a party called the Patriotic Front, and the bush war against the white population over which they are presiding is spreading from the border area into the rest of the country. People are afraid, and an exodus of whites appears to be beginning. They must be feeling desperate, although most of our friends over there still say they are determined to preserve their country, and their lives. And me? I am fast losing hope of any acceptable solution to the problem.

We are going home for Christmas, and then what?

Some Facts About Libya

Libya is a country in North Africa on the Mediterranean coast. It is divided into three main areas: Tripolitania, Cyrenaica, and Fezzan. The land consists mostly of desert, with a narrow coastal plain rising to the Tibetsi Mountains along the southern border. The population is chiefly of Berber and Arab origin.

This area was a very important part of the Roman Empire and the ruins of the ancient Roman cities of Sabratha and Leptis Magna are wonderful reminders of this. During the sixteenth century Libya was under Turkish domination. In 1912 it was annexed by Italy, and there are still signs of Italian influence. It was the scene of heavy fighting during World War 2 and the Italians were driven out by the Allies in 1943. Following this defeat Libya came under the control of France and the United Kingdom.

The modern history of independent Libya began in 1951. The country declared its independence on December 24th of that year. The United Kingdom of Libya was formed and Mohammed Idris, the Emir of Cyrenaica, was declared King of Libya. He was known as King Idris.

Between 1959 and 1970 considerable prospecting for oil took place during which major deposits were found. Libya is now one of the world's largest oil producers, and this makes up about 98% of the country's exports. Liquefied natural gas is also exported. Oil has turned the territory into a rich country.

Subsistence agriculture still takes place, but the arid soil restricts crop production to the narrow coastal areas and scattered oases. Small amounts of barley and wheat are grown, and there are also olives and dates. Livestock farming of sheep, goats and cattle are the main agricultural occupations. Nobody seems sure of the origin of the Berber tribes, but some of these people are nomadic, wandering from place to place across the desert from one oasis to another. They are friendly people, and the ones I met during a trip to the little desert town of Ghadames laughed and tried to communicate, and one of the ladies gave me a pretty bead bracelet she had made, and she refused absolutely to take any money for it.

Manufacture is limited to local crafts such as bead work, basket making and home made textile goods. The official language of the country is Arabic, but English and Italian are also spoken.

The United Kingdom of Libya came to an end on September 1st 1969 when a group of military officers led by Col. Muammar Gadaffi staged a coup d'etat against King Idris, who was exiled to Egypt. The new regime abolished the monarchy and proclaimed the Libyan Arab Republic. Gadaffi emerged as leader of the Revolutionary Command Council and eventually the de facto head of state, which he still is. He pledged himself to take an active role in the Palestinian/Arab cause, promote Arab Unity, and encourage social justice and the equitable distribution of wealth. He abolished all foreign military installations from Libya, he expelled several thousand Italian residents, and by 1971 libraries and cultural centres operated by foreign governments were ordered closed. Gadaffi rejected both Eastern Communism and Western Capitalism and claimed he was charting an independent course.

In 1973 Gadaffi introduced a Cultural Revolution based on Islamic principals. Libya is firmly against the existance of Israel and stands accused of causing terrorist measures abroad including involvement in the Lockerbie disaster. There is a total ban on alcohol and other non-Islamic practices. No tolerance of "difference" exists. Gadaffi has turned the country into an uncomfortable place to live and work for non Muslims. Despite the possible tourist attractions of the well-excavated ruins of the old Roman cities, and miles of beautiful sandy beaches, and guaranteed hot summer weather, visitors are not encouraged in Libya. After a battle, it is possible to obtain a visitor's visa, but such visitors are allocated a Libyan 'minder' who accompanies them wherever they go and watches every movement. In these circumstances one has to be dedicated to acquiring an extraordinary experience at any cost. Nonetheless, we have friends who have made it into Libya and at least found it interesting.

Nine

Abu Dhabi 1976–1981

February 1978

Dear Ruth,

It is time I wrote a letter to you, but you will know from my note inside last year's Christmas card that we are now in Abu Dhabi. Let me go back to the end of 1975, when we moved from Hertford to the house we bought in Sawtry, a village between Cambridge and Peterborough, in order to be closer to the children's schools. The house was new and there was some tidying up to be done before it was ready for the festive season, but we celebrated Christmas 1975 in Fen Lane, Sawtry. Here is a snapshot of us gathered there, myself and the three children, Grandma McKee (my mother), my friend Geraldine and her son. Jim took the photograph.

At this time Jim was preparing for his new posting to Abu Dhabi in the United Arab Emirates, and it has turned out to be a wonderful place to live. Of course it is a Muslim country, but it is nothing at all like Libya. Jim complains that I am unfair to the ordinary Libyans, who were kindly and pleasant. Jim is right, but Gadafi's tyranny completely wipes out most of the positive memories. The Emirates seem to be ruled by a group of benign sheiks, and they are all very tolerant of our western ways. We can walk around in western clothes, drink alcoholic beverages, women are free to do as they wish: drive cars, swim in bikinis, be seen out with men other than their husbands, and, by and large, do anything with which they feel

Family at Christmas

On the dunes

At The Club – Abu Dhabi

comfortable. I would not walk around the souk in anything other than modest dress, but that is my choice, and most of us feel the same way.

After Libya it is so good to have all the freedoms we are used to having. The alcohol situation is quite amusing. Clearly, there is a feeling that there should be some kind of regulation so they have created liquor stores manned by a British firm called Gray McKenzie. Non Muslims are given a liquor licence based on the salary of the person concerned. Since most people hereabouts get very good salaries, and drink is not expensive, the ration is more than generous, it is HUGE. Even though we give many dinner parties, and drink unreservedly, we cannot get through our monthly allowance. One of the nicest and most disarming things about it is that where a Muslim has a European wife she is given half the allowance her husband would have received had he been a non Muslim. What remarkable generosity of spirit!

We live in a large house in a residential suburb called Batin, amongst people most of whom work for one British-controlled company or another. Many of them have children away at school in England, as we do. The younger children attend the Al Khubarat School here, which provides primary education for English-speaking children the majority of whom are British. Jeremy was four when we arrived here and the company had already acquired a school place for him and paid the fees. It is a good school, although, again, it provides morning school only. He has made lots of friends, likes going to school, and seems to be coming along well.

We have a whole new way of life out here, different and enjoyable. Abu Dhabi is surrounded by desert and the children find it great fun to climb to the top of a sand dune and then slide down again like a human sleigh. One of the photographs I am sending shows them sitting with me on the summit of one of the dunes.

We belong to 'The Club', and our social life centres around it. Membership is expensive but most British companies, including I.A.L, pay the membership fees. The Club has a lot to offer. It has a private beach, a big swimming pool, facilities for a range of sports, including tennis, badminton, squash, and sailing. Jeremy has swimming lessons and soon became a good swimmer; he is beginning to collect swimming awards and these have to be sewn on to his little swimming trunks. The Club also has a splendid restaurant, a large bar, and another, smaller outside bar beside the pool, a club lounge, and a relatively good library. I do a weekly stint helping to run the library. There is a paid Manager and Manageress who live on the premises, and there are paid cooks, waiters and bar staff. Muslims are not supposed to consume alcohol but some of them do, and they appear to like our dissolute European ways. Most weeks there is a film shown in the open air. The restaurant staff cook and serve very good meals, including a traditional British Christmas dinner on Christmas day. You can buy fine wines to go with it at low prices because there are no taxes.

As well as all this I have a full time job here. Briefly, I was a dental receptionist, but now I work for a doctor, a gynaecologist who works mainly as a GP but also does antenatal care for the oil companies. The doctor, Mitzi, is Armenian and speaks fluent Arabic, and that is useful. I make appointments, keep the records, send out the bills, and am a general gofer. I work all morning, and then go back for the evening surgery. I also sometimes interview infertile British women who are thinking about the adoption option because I can put them in touch with appropriate adoption agencies in England.

Mitzi and her husband Peter soon became good friends, and on Fridays, which is our (the Muslim) day off, we usually go out on their motor boat with them, trawling for fish, snorkelling amongst the coral, spear fishing, and sometimes visiting an island in the Gulf, and occasionally camping on Ras al Gharab or Rabbit Island. I am not too keen on the camping, but the children love it and the whole boating experience is wonderful for them. Laurence does sailing at school, but none of them have ever had the opportunity to mess about in boats on the sea. It is very hot in this country, and water sports are therefore welcome. They have also tried water skiing at The Club and sailing on sailing boats belonging to our friends. Fortunately they are all competent swimmers.

Laurence and Penelope are sitting in front of the tent we had to buy for these occasions.

We have, too, visited most of the other Emirates just to have a look. Dubai is bigger than Abu Dhabi, and some people think better, but I am happy to be where we are. The others are smaller, but they offer similar things. We have spent a Christmas in Fujeira, explored Khor Forkhan, and stayed in Sharjah and Dubai because we have friends there. We have also made several trips to the interesting little desert town of Al Ain, and once we were taken by helicopter to Lima Oasis to the retreat of one of the Sheiks. These trips make a nice change from routine, although really there is not a lot of routine in our lives anyway. We are happy and busy doing lots of different things, and we are very lucky to be here. It more than makes up for the new and nasty changes we had to face in Africa, and our eventual need to leave that continent. One of the pictures I enclose is of Jim on the beach at Khor Forkhan. He had just found a piece of jetsam from a boat and it looked as if it had his name on it.

Africa. Yes, we still watch from afar what is happening there, and it is all very sad. Zambia is increasingly dogged by tribulations due to economic mismanagement, debt, corruption, disease, and impoverishment. Malawi has comparable problems under the eccentric despot Dr Banda.

Camping on Ras al Gharab

Camping on Ras al Gharab

Jeremy in Pafos showing his prowess at spear fishing

Coral in the Arabian Gulf. It is amongst this that the good swimmers amongst us, including Jeremy, do their fishing with spear guns.

We had many happy years living in both these countries and it is with dismay that we are watching them slide into hopeless poverty.

Rhodesia, however, is the saddest case of all because Ian Smith's antecedents worked their guts out to build it, suffering hardship, sorrow, disease, and lots of other problems. It took them many years to complete the project, but they did it. Out of raw African bushveld they created a successful European-style society with modern cities, a thriving economy, a well-run administration and competent government. I shall never forget how astonished I was in the early 1960s to come across such a country in the middle of Africa. Is this great achievement to be slowly throttled by forces beyond the control of the present proficient rulers? That is the way it looks. The bush war has spread to the borders of Salisbury and the security situation is desperate. By the beginning of last year Smith was beginning to capitulate and when Henry Kissinger, the American Secretary of State, with the agreement of Britain, presented him with a draft settlement providing for majority rule within two years he agreed to it, with certain conditions to protect the interests of the white people. The black nationalists would not accept it. The whites were shocked and bewildered and thousands of them left their homeland with hope that they could start again elsewhere. During the year the slogan 'one-man-one-vote' became a battle cry, and the militants are getting ever more militant. The writing is on the wall, as they say, and it is greatly distressing. But of course we are observing these happenings from far-away Abu Dhabi, which helps to cushion the blow.

November 1979

Dear Ruth,

We are approaching the end of another year, and it has been a good one for us. I hope you will be able to say the same. We continue to enjoy life in Abu Dhabi, with all its advantages. Added to this, we have recently bought a holiday flat in Pafos, Cyprus, because we wanted to acquire a place in the sun before we were priced out of the market. Cyprus is not far from Abu Dhabi. She is just beginning to recover from the Turkish invasion of 1974. The north of the island was taken over by the Turks, and the Greek Cypriots who lived there were driven from their homes and have become refuges in the south. Apartments and houses are being built at a rate of knots and they are relatively cheap. The Cypriots are planning to develop the tourist industry as well as re-settle the refuges, and we don't know how that will pan out, but we enjoy our flat very much. It is a super place to go for a holiday, and a visit to Pafos breaks up the long summer vacation very nicely. I enclose a photo of Jeremy in Pafos showing his prowess at spear fishing.

1981

We were in Abu Dhabi until 1981, and then, sadly and reluctantly, we left. The United Arab Emirates took on the staffing and management of their own communication systems. They offered Jim a job with them, and oh how I wish we had accepted the offer. But Jim had a permanent and pensionable post with IAL and we were thinking in terms of what we then imagined was a guaranteed future, free from impoverishment.

Jim and the children left Abu Dhabi sooner than I did because I had a few ends to tie up at work, Before I left this very agreeable location I heard that we had been posted for a second tour in Libya, an appalling fate. I was despondent.

Some Facts About The United Arab Emirates

The United Arab Emirates are a federation of sheikdoms in the Middle East on the south coast of the Arabian Gulf and the Gulf of Oman. They border Oman and Saudi Arabia. The sheikdoms used

Jim and Me – our last boat trip on 'Given Life'

Jim with Jetsam with his name on it

to be called the Trucial States. They consist of Abu Dhabi, Dubai, Fujeira, Ajman, Ras al Khaima, Sharjah and Um al Qaiwain. A political treaty with Britain in 1892 made the Trucial States a protectorate and British troops were stationed there until independence on 2nd December 1971. Then they became the United Arab Emirates and a member of the United Nations. The native population of the UAE is Arab and their religion is Sunnite Muslim. The official language is Arabic. The land is flat, sandy desert.

In the early 1960s oil was discovered in Abu Dhabi and this led to a call for quick unification by the other sheikdoms. Fishing and pearl gathering are still practised but the oil of Abu Dhabi and Dubai both underground and offshore is the chief product and export. This has turned the Emirates into a very rich country, and they have evolved into a modern high income nation.

Almost three quarters of the population of the Emirates is made up of non citizens. It includes a huge number of male migrant workers and this has brought about an unnatural sex distribution. There are twice as many males as females, the highest of any nation in the world. The high living standards and economic opportunities make the country an attractive destination for foreigners. There are lots of Pakistanis and Bangladeshis working in the constructive industry, many British and Americans in the oil industry, or running import/export and other businesses. There are Indians, Sri Lankans, Filipinos and others adding to the numbers. Many thousands of Palestinians live there too, a lot of them as political refugees. There are also a fair number from other Gulf Arab states, such as Egyptians, Somalis, and Sudanese who have adopted the native customs and culture. Women can apply for jobs the same as anybody else, but are less likely to get them except in designated female-type jobs. The UAE does not allow economic migrants to remain in the country without a job. Individuals past retirement age must return to their countries of origin, as must anybody who loses his job. People found to have TB, Hepatitis or Aids are also promptly deported.

The large cities of Abu Dhabi and Dubai have grown into enormous conurbations full of skyscrapers, modern buildings and wonderful shopping centres, and visitors to these cities flow regularly in and out, especially to Dubai.

The Emirates have both secular and Islamic law for civil, criminal and high courts. The country tries to present a public image of tolerance, but it stands accused of discrimination and human rights abuses. In a basically Arab culture I do not see how this can be otherwise. To expect a Muslim country to accept western ideas of political correctness, a somewhat hypocritical concept anyway, is just too much to imagine. For instance, the form of Shiria law exercised prohibits sodomy and thus outlaws blatant homosexual practices. Sex on the beach and homosexual behaviour in public is likely to lead to imprisonment, and then deportation. As for homosexual marriage, the mind just boggles. Homosexual Arabs in the Emirates must be discreet about it, and one knows that there are many groups in our own country too who do not embrace Political Man.

They do not 'do' public prosecutions in the Emirates and I do not know if Shiria Law for them includes execution of women for adultery, but I cannot easily imagine it. I worked in Abu Dhabi for a woman gynaecologist. Once a week she ran a surgery especially for ladies, and thus, in the course of my work I met many Arab women from the Hareems. They took off their veils in female company, many spoke fluent English, and I gained the impression that in their way they exercised a lot of power. Some even ran small businesses. They did not actually work in a shop, but they kept the books and were the power behind the scene. They seemed content with the way things were for them and in no way appeared intimidated or brow-beaten. One of the things the doctor was called upon to do occasionally was to repair a hyman the day before a wedding night, which suggests some women were not as chaste as they were supposed to be.

Yes, there is discrimination in the workplace. This is because of the system in place for migrant workers. Each employee must be sponsored by a local Arab citizen, and each sponsor is responsible for his employees. He is supposed to supply them with housing, wages, and health care. It is up to the employee to negotiate his wages with the employer. Prospective employers will specify religion, nationality and sex and it is usual to have different pay scales depending on nationality and sex, sometimes based on the salary a worker might get in his own country. It is usual for employers to hold the passports of their workers, although this is supposed to be illegal. Some workers just come along and sell their labour cheaply, but are deported if they are caught. The government has ignored international pressure to introduce trade unions despite repeated promises to do so.

All these violations of 'Human Rights' are true by modern secular standards, but is it possible, or desirable, to interfere with the culture, customs, and religion of this Muslim Arab country? The UAE appears to be doing its best to adapt to the demands and expectations of a twenty-first century democracy. Any change in their native customs will, or may, evolve slowly as time moves on.

We lived very happily in the Emirates as a Western European family for more than five years. and we have never stopped regretting that we did not stay there until Jim retired, when we would of course have been deported to our country of origin. Perhaps we Westerners have something to learn from the United Arab Emirates about Economic Migrants.

Ten

Endings 1981–1983

I have finished writing down the information I shared with Ruth and which I extracted from the letters she sent back to me. The last letter was dated 1981. She wanted me to leave a record of our story for my descendants so that they could view it through the eyes of some of the people who were there during this epoch, first and foremost through the eyes of their own ancestors. What I have written so far is exactly as I saw it at that time, though I have peppered the missive with more photographs than I actually sent to Ruth because I think the offspring of our grandchildren and great grandchildren would like to see how we looked in those old days. It adds colour to the written word, even though the photographs are in black and white. It was not until the later years of the twentieth century that the general public were able to buy clever cameras.

What I write now, at the end of 2008, has to be dragged up through the mists of time, and my memory may be selective. Some things I can clearly recall, but there are other things I must have forgotten.

The End of Overseas Family Postings

Our second tour in Libya began in the first part of 1981. Libya was worse than it had ever been. Gadafi had closed all small businesses, mainly shops, and founded state-run supermarkets that seldom had eatable food. One day there might be a shelf of biscuits, on another day perhaps tins of sardines. The staff were surly, and refused to give change.

If you didn't have the correct money they pocketed the rest. We could often get vegetables and eggs and bread from illegal traders. If one could deal with a live chicken one could sometimes purchase one from a villager, but I had no idea how to operate on the innards of a fowl and I did not wish to learn. Meat was available when it came in, but it was not sent for charity and the government often failed to pay its debts. I remember one evening watching a boatload of live cattle, an export from some place overseas, turn round and go back because the company that sent it remained unpaid. We did, however, manage to get a goose for Christmas. It was a fiend to cook because the fat had to be constantly drained off, but it was delicious to eat, particularly as we had been on a food shortage diet for some time. Most of us lost a considerable amount of weight, even me, who appeared to have no weight to lose. I remember this period when, today, people are fretting about obesity, and scientists keep looking for a guilty gene because they think there must be something in their genetic inheritance that makes some people tend towards fatness. I also look back on the mal-nourished children I helped in Zambia, and the people in Europe who were starving during World War Two, and those who stumbled out of concentration camps when the war ended. There was not a single fat person amongst them. Could it be that modern-day problems are entirely caused by greedy mouths bearing down on excessive amounts of needless food? But I digress. The worst thing that happened during this spell in Libya was when we had to battle for visas to be granted to the children so that they could come home for the Christmas holidays. We couldn't get a visa for them to come, and we couldn't get a visa for me to leave. They were stranded in an airport hotel while the company in London struggled with the problem. I went bananas. It was the only time in my life I have ever taken valium. Eventually one of the senior managers in London doled out a bribe to a Libyan official, also in London, and he issued the visas. The trio arrived just in time for Christmas, all beaming broadly and apparently none the worse for their adventure.

Nevertheless there were some positive things about this period in Libya. For a while I even had a part-time job as an assistant accountant with an American oil company, working out salaries and tax for the oily boys as they went to and from their homes in the United States. The children were older now and they took more interest in the fascinating remains of Roman Libya, especially Penelope, who was doing classical studies at school. Here they are, sitting side by side on the communal Roman loos at Leptis Magna and laughing at the public nature of these facilities.

I also took an excursion with six American wives, who's husbands worked in the desert for an oil company. We went to Ghadames to visit the cave dwellings of early nomadic tribes. We stayed in a nearby village with basic loos but very good food!

We were also able to visit the Skanska Camp, which was a compound provided by a Danish company for its staff who worked in Tripoli. It had a swimming pool that we enjoyed, and the company also sent out food for the workers and we could buy delicious Danish sandwiches for lunch. In addition, the beautiful, unspoiled, empty beaches were still there to be freely used by anyone with the inclination to do so. Therefore life in Libya was not all bad. There was worse to come, but we were certainly not sorry to leave Tripoli in 1983 when our contract there ended. By this time we had moved to a flat in Cambridge city, and we went back there, as usual not knowing where we would be sent next. We were not yet aware there would be no more overseas family postings.

It was not long before we found out. IAL was losing telecommunications contracts all over the world as countries began to recruit staff for themselves rather than doing it through a foreign company. Moreover Jim was now in his fifties and this was considered more or less retiring age for permanent staff in foreign countries. Disastrously, he was

At Leptis Magna, Libya

At Leptis Magna, Libya

At Leptis Magna, Libya   *Caves at Ghadames*

Village near Ghadames

posted to Wales. This was calamitous for us because we had three children at expensive independent schools, and with Jim working in Wales we no longer qualified for help with school fees. Penelope and Laurence, or Larry, as he had come to be known, were both studying for 'O' level exams and good results in these were necessary in order to go on to 'A' level and subsequently to higher education. Jeremy was at the King's School, Ely, where he was doing well. He had only been at Kimbolton for a very short time when we were informed that the boarding house for the prep. was to be closed. It happened suddenly, and we had been given no prior warning. For a year he was boarded out in a large Roman Catholic family, but he was not Catholic and in many ways seemed to be the odd one out. We swiftly explored the possibilities of Bishop's Stortford and King's. and the coin came down in favour of Kings. While he was at the King's School he sang as a chorister in the cathedral, he learned the flute, he was in the appropriate school cricket team, he had just passed the 11+ exam which would give him a grammar school place in counties where they still had them, he was happy there, but he was still only twelve years old. Where did we go from here? How would we find the money to complete the task we began, to educate our children as well as their ability and interests allowed them to be educated?

The End of our Child-Rearing Years: a précis of the next decade.

Jim's IAL posting to Wales brought about cataclysmic change in our circumstances. We could not meet all our commitments on the salary he earned. I could and would work too, but that would not bring in enough financial backing to deal with the problem. If Jim left IAL our pension at the end of the day would be abysmally small, even supposing he could find a more lucrative job. We were faced with a conundrum.

Jim in Jeddah 1988

*Jeremy at King's
before a cricket match*

What should we do? It was a challenge that required colonial-style economic management and adroit administration. It would involve decisive negotiation, forward-planning, getting the priorities right, a certain manipulation of the system, and downright hard work. Well, we both had plenty of management experience in those old days of imposing western civilisation and progress on Africa, so we rolled up our sleeves and got on with it. It was 1983, and we had at least ten years more child-rearing years ahead of us. These are the things we did.

First, Jim found an unaccompanied overseas post in the Middle East with another company, Cable and Wireless. The pay was good, and because he was on 'bachelor' status he received free board and lodging in the mess. He worked out that if the job lasted for long enough, he could save sufficient money to overcome the loss of pension rights, to pay school fees for Laurence and Penelope for the next four years, and to see all three of them through university. These were our top priorities, and he took the post. It was on contract, with a four month stint overseas followed by a month or so at home. His first posting was to Doha, then to Saudi Arabia, to Dahran, then to Jeddah, and finally to Riyadh. His contract was renewed from year to year. He was in Riyadh at the time of the first Gulf War in 1992, maintaining the communications system for the National Guard, and he received a medal for his pains. There was a blip in 1994 when Cable and Wireless decided to get rid of staff over sixty and he had to work in England (for Phillips} for a while, but then he got another contract to work in Saudi Arabia, and he worked there until 1997, when he reached the age of 65 and retired.

Second, I went back to full-time social work in England. I acquired a job with Lincolnshire County Council early in 1984, and we moved to a village called Pinchbeck, near Spalding. I didn't fall in love with Lincolnshire. It is very rural and it seemed seemed rather slow after the bustle and stimulation of Cambridge. But I worked very hard, often including weekends and evenings, so there was not much time to do anything else. Our Pinchbeck house was big enough to accommodate guests and sometimes it was full of visiting boys. Penelope's school friends mostly lived in Lincolnshire anyway. I had a lovely neighbour called Shirley who I employed to help with the domestic chores, and she was wonderful, doing far more than she need have done, including keeping an eye on the youngsters when they were on vacation and I was not there, and even taking my skirts to her mother who was good at sewing and was able to take them in at the waist so that they were a better fit. I have always been on the thin side.

As I said earlier, Lincolnshire still had grammar schools and Jeremy had passed the exam. qualifying for a place in one. Lincolnshire even had a grammar school with a boarding house, which would be useful if ever I decided to visit Jim in the Middle East. I didn't because I was very busy, and there was always a hassle over getting visas in Saudi Arabia. However, very reluctantly, we moved Jeremy from the King's School, Ely, to Caistor Grammar School. He often came home for weekends if I were not working, and he settled down there with typical good humour. The school lacked the extra-curricula activities that King's had on offer, and he missed his cricket team. But the maths. master, Peter Taylor, had coached a table tennis team at the school and it did well in the Lincolnshire League. Jeremy became good at table tennis and was selected for the team. He also took quite big parts in the school plays The academic standards at the school were reasonably high, and in due course he got the required number of GCSEs (as O Level was now called) at good grades, and thus he qualified to go on to A level. Meanwhile Laurence and Penelope had already finished the A level course (1985), and both were now at university, Larry at Sheffield and Penny at Keble College, Oxford. I had lost the battle to keep the names we gave them at birth, and Penny and Larry they had become.

During 1987 Jeremy, still working for GCSE, began to talk wildly of wanting to rent accommodation in the town next year, instead of boarding at the school while he worked for his A levels. He said it was because he wanted to go out with his friends in the evenings. Hmmm…. I smelt danger. He had always been a well-behaved child, never in the least unruly, but he was 16 years old, and I didn't want to clash horns with him over this, a request he thought perfectly rational. I decided, therefore, the answer would be for him to live at home. I knew that Hills Road Sixth Form College in Cambridge was an excellent school and it achieved results second to none. 'Right', I said to myself, 'that is where he will go'. The snags were, first one must be resident in Cambridge, and second, just about every parent with an able sixteen-year-old wanted him or her to go to Hills Road, unless the offspring were already attending independent schools with their own sixth forms. Cambridge is a breeding ground for able children and therefore Hills Road was vastly over-subscribed. Jeremy would have to compete for a place. However, there was another Sixth Form College in Cambridge, less pushy, and with less overpowering success, but it was not a bad second best. I put this option to Jeremy, and he readily agreed to it. Thus I set about arranging to keep my part of the bargain. I discussed the proposal with Jim and he was happy about it, and so we sold our Pinchbeck House and, in March 1987 we moved back to Cambridge, I must say with some relief. Cambridge is a lovely city.

We moved into a newish village called Bar Hill. I got a job with Barnardos in London helping to run the Counselling Services Project. It was only three days a week, but once we had settled in I added another part-time job with the then East Anglia Child Care and Adoption Society. Later I worked for a while in Cambridgeshire Social Services Department. Jeremy's GCSE results were good and he was

Caistor Table Tennis Team with Trophies. Jeremy is second on the left, holding his trophy the wrong way round.

A Cambridge Scene

granted a place at Hills Road Sixth Form College. I still found him an easy child, adolescent now. He even earned his own pocket money during the first year by working at a roadside restaurant called the Little Chef at weekends. In the second year A levels became more pressing. But he liked to have a good time and every now and then he was in trouble with his tutor for not working hard enough on his assignments. Nonetheless he did well in his A levels and earned his place at Reading University, where he went in 1990. Penelope and Laurence both graduated in 1988.

One thing that did not end in 1983 were holidays in our Cyprus flat. During these years I had many pleasurable visits to our Pafos apartment, sometimes with the whole family, sometimes with the children, who occasionally brought friends, sometimes with my own friends, and sometimes with Jim, or on my own. Also, we lent it rent-free to various associates who liked to go there. They only had to pay their own bills, and they looked after it for us, and put right anything that had gone wrong in between our own holidays there. The flat gave great value for money, and we were well-pleased with it. We had a small home in Pafos for twenty-five years, and in that time we only moved once, to a new apartment in Chloraka, a coastal village a short distance from the town. This was because the tourist industry developed and expanded rapidly, as intended, to replace the tourist industry that had been centred around Famagusta on the other side of the border. Our flat in Kato Pafos was right in the centre of the tourist area and became noisy and full of revelry which shattered the peace of the night. We had to move away. At this time we were planning to eventually retire to Cyprus, but later, after we discovered how cold it could be in winter, and how ferocious were the winter storms, we decided to keep it as a place for extended holidays. We sold the flat towards the end of 2004 and after that made long visits in rented accommodation. Finally, due to old age and declining health, our visits became limited to short holidays in hotels.

Some Facts About Cyprus

Cyprus is tucked away in the eastern corner of the Mediterranean Sea. It has a history fraught with battles, conquests and drama dating back to the Neolithic period 5,800 BC. There was already a Greek colony on the island 4,000 years ago. Throughout the following ages many different Empires held sway over Cyprus. Phoenicians, Assyrians, Egyptians and Persians all had their day. Then along came the Romans in 58 BC and they were in charge for several centuries, followed by the Byzantines, Lusignans and Venetians. In 1570 attack by the Turks brought Cyprus under the Ottoman Empire and Turkey reigned for 300 years. I guess it was during this period that Turkish Cypriots became a large minority group on the island. The British took over the administration of Cyprus in 1878, and in 1925 it became a Crown Colony.

Because of its historical past the population of Cyprus is truly a mix of many backgrounds and cultures, but by the time Britain took over it was divided into Greek Cypriots and Turkish Cypriots, with the Greeks forming a big majority. The early history of Cyprus is well documented in books written by scholarly historians, of which I am not one. However, it is helpful to know briefly what happened during the twentieth century in order to understand the political situation in Cyprus today because this permeates almost every aspect of life in Cyprus. By the 1930s Greek Cypriots were advocating union with Greece – Enosis, and this became their ambition. Even now that is what many of them would like. But they also wanted independence from Britain and in 1955 a Greek Cypriot organisation, EOKA, led by Archbishop Makarios and General Grivas began guerrilla warfare against the British. It was a nasty conflict. Cyprus became a republic in 1960 and a member of the Commonwealth in 1961, but, by agreement, Britain still owns two military bases on the south coast and the influence of

In Cyprus

In Cyprus

In Cyprus – Kourion

In Cyprus

Britain remains strong. Most Cypriots speak good English, driving is on the left, road signs and public notices are written in Greek and English, and the afternoon tea ritual is to be found all over southern Cyprus.

After independence the struggle for union with Greece continued and the demand became increasingly persistent. In 1963 inter-communal violence broke out, sponsored by both Greece and Turkey. The United Nations became involved and in 1964 a United Nations peace-keeping force was sent to Cyprus. and it is still there. General Grivas ran a terrorist campaign in favour of Enosis until he died in 1974. In that year, 1974, the Greek junta, disenchanted with the policy of Makarios in Cyprus and the failure to progress towards Enosis, organised a coup on 13th July and declared Cyprus's Union with Greece. Turkey objected and 7 days later invaded Cyprus. The Greek forces were outnumbered and could not resist the attack. Thus around 170,000 Greek Cypriots were driven from their homes in the north and fled to the south, while around 50,000 Turkish Cypriots fled in the opposite direction. The result was the partition of the island, with almost 40% of the land now in the Turkish occupation zone. The Turks set up their own government in the north, which did not get international recognition. Nevertheless in 1983 the Turkish north declared itself an independent state as the Turkish Republic of Northern Cyprus. This was, and is, only recognised by Turkey. Reunification talks have been held time and time again since 1974, so far without reaching agreement. Cyprus remains a divided island. Since the partition of the Republic, the north and south of Cyprus have gone their separate ways. But it is a de facto partition, not a de jure partition, and therefore when Cyprus became a member of the European Union in 2004 it was as The Republic of Cyprus, and it included the whole island. This is a very strange situation in view of the fact that partition is the reality position. It impinges on life in Cyprus and anyone visiting the island is immediately made aware of it.

Cyprus likes to be known as Aphrodite's island. In Greek mythology Aphrodite was the Goddess of Love, called Venus by the

Romans. She is said to have risen from the foam and emerged from the sea on a beach near Pafos. She is described as very beautiful, and Cyprus is basically a most beautiful island. Kissed by the sun, circled by the clear blue waters of the sea, it has a magic that draws people back time and again. Geographically it is a land of contrasts. It has fine sandy beaches, cliffs rising up from the sea, mountain ranges with rugged peaks and fertile valleys. In the spring there are a big variety of wild flowers, some of them found only in Cyprus. There is an abundance of bird life on the island. The Ornithological Society has counted more than 700 species, many f them migratory. Consequently there are a goodly number of twitchers creeping around with binoculars dangling from their necks. With its long and varied history Cyprus is full of archaeological treasures. Every time a spade is dug into the ground new discoveries come to light. Most excavations have been carried out on sites of the Roman Empire, and the remains of Roman cities can be viewed at Kourion near Limassol and on smaller sites elsewhere.

Most Greek Cypriots are members of the Orthodox Church of Cyprus, one of the oldest Christian churches in the world, having been founded by the apostles Paul and Barnabus when they landed in Cyprus in 45 AD. Turkish Cypriots are mainly Muslim but very liberal and westernised in their views and behaviour.

Agriculture used to be the main source of employment. The Cypriots grew and sold bananas, melons, and other tropical fruits, grain crops, grapes, potatoes and assorted vegetables, olives, carobs, almonds, walnuts and many other products. However, after the Turkish invasion there was a need to rebuild the economy and to replace the traditional tourist centre of Verosha in Famagusta on the other side of the island from which the Greek owners fled. Varosha is now a decayed ghost town of crumbling buildings, broken roads and prolific thick undergrowth. The development of the new tourist industry was highly successful. It grew like Topsy, and Southern Cyprus developed a flourishing economy, at huge cost to the environment. Most of the beautiful coastal areas were turned into a concrete jungle of hotels, holiday apartments, and villas in the sun for foreigners, mostly British, restaurants, tavernas, discos, night clubs and more, much more, and cheap foreign labour is a big part of the scene, replacing the cheerful family-run businesses of the past.

Cyprus handicrafts are still to be seen, though less so than before. They include basket-making, ceramics, weaving, lace-making crochet work, pottery and other skills, although, as in many other places, goods made in China predominate in the tourist markets. It is well worth going up into the mountains and exploring some of the mountain villages where the 'old' Cyprus can still be found.

There is still a lot to see and do in Cyprus, catering for all sorts of interests and needs, and there are many tourist guides with suggestions about where to go and what to do, according to your interests. It is worth reading one of them before you begin your visit.

As I write this at the beginning of 2009 problems have arisen because of the current global recession. The pound sterling which was once worth nearly two euros is now worth only one, and expensive holidays are more difficult to afford. Fewer and fewer people can manage to buy homes in the sun and the property market is flooded with unsold houses and flats. Some British residents can no longer sustain the lifestyle in Cyprus. In many cases incomes have been halved by the fall in value of the British pound, yet prices of goods and services are steadily rising, and there are no welfare hand-outs in Cyprus. It looks as if a period of hardship is on the way.

And Finally...

Time passed. Jeremy graduated in 1993. Our child-rearing task was almost finished. The children were now reasonably well-educated young people and we hoped they were ready for the final launch into this difficult and iniquitous world with the ability to fend for themselves, and to continue learning the things they wanted or needed to know. Now it was up to them.

We have grown old. Growing old is a great misfortune, and it is very nasty indeed. At the end of 1994 we decided to set ourselves up in a little home that could be easily managed in our retirement years, with no garden to look after, no lawns to mow, and small enough to make sure the domestics were not too onerous. Therefore we bought a pint-sized flat in Milton, on the edge of Cambridge city, in a pleasant little Close surrounded by lawns and trees which were looked after by a gardener. Jeremy was not quite ready for his final launch so he lived with us for a time. He was doing a teacher training course at Christ's College, a qualification that he used only briefly.

Soon after this came the wake-up calls. Early in 1995 I had a stroke and for a while lost the ability to speak, write, and swallow. This was the introduction to my retirement. I had to give up work, but I eventually recovered well from the stroke, and I started to spend a lot more time in Cyprus. Next I began to get frequent chest infections. Emphysema was diagnosed, together with related lung conditions which go under the umbrella name of COPD. I felt aggrieved because I had never in my life smoked. Nobody could tell what had caused this lung disease but it was put down to childhood illnesses, and passive smoking through being with people who smoked. The third wake-up call was the nastiest of all.

Jeremy

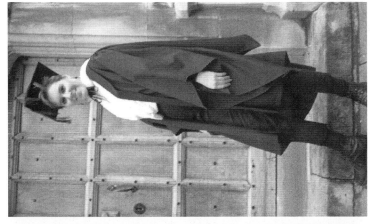

Penelope

Graduation

Laurence

Jeremy, Penelope & Laurence

Mary, the bike and the babies

Jim and Pam at Cherry Close.

Jeremy at Cherry Close.

I had a detached retina in 2007 which caused me to lose my sight in the left eye, and since I have very poor vision in the other eye, I am now partially blind. I have become a frail old lady, and I do not like it at all.

When Jim retired in 1997 we began to spend around seven months of the year in our Pafos apartment, enjoying the sunny climate and the general good humour and cheerful company and get-togethers of British expats. However, eventually we became too old and ailing to join in the activities we once enjoyed, and managing two homes became more difficult. Furthermore, by the time we moved into the twenty-first century rowdy, high-spirited holiday makers had taken over most of the coastline, lots of cheap foreign labour was employed to staff many of the old family tavernas, and British immigration was so vast that in some cases expatriates outnumbered Greeks. Because of all these changes we decided to come home. It was the end of an extended and happy chapter of our lives. For several years after that we continued to travel a lot. We went to Singapore, Malaysia, Thailand, South Africa, and to many places in Europe, including plenty of return visits to Pafos. We have a lot of friends who live in Cyprus, and after 30+ years of coming and going to that little island it is difficult to break the link, and, despite the increasing grottiness of parts of the region, we still get pleasure from it. We especially enjoy going up into the mountains to unspoiled places, where the donkey still exists, where the village taverna is still owned and run by a local family, and where we find reminders of the old Cyprus.

Jim remains reasonably fit for his age, but he has recently had a total knee replacement, and of course he is nowhere near as agile as he once was. We are both past our use-by date, and there it is. We potter about in the flat, go to a variety of classes and lectures run by the U3A in Cambridge, and look forward to the comings and goings of our children and grandchildren. Larry has a wonderful wife, Mary, who can often be seen cycling around in Cambridge with her two little boys, one in the front and one on the back. It looks perilous.

Penny and her partner Robert also have two little boys. Jeremy and his girlfriend Haley live together but have no children. Jeremy observes his siblings coping with child care concerns and finds the prospect too daunting.

We were Economic Migrants for most of our working lives. However, during our intermittent spells in UK along the way we managed to fit satisfactorily into the local scene, although we did not like it. It is not difficult with three children. There are the schools, the children's friends and their parents, the neighbours, the local community, and our own friends. We never made a secret of the fact that we preferred a warmer climate and the comfortable lifestyle working overseas offered. Many people thought we were crazy, but they accepted our strange ways, and we have never regretted any of it.

We always knew we must return home one day and so here we are. We are old now, with many of the ailments this brings along. Being old is awful. But we have our children and grandchildren here, and all our old friends who have survived this far, for me dating back to my schooldays long, long ago. Reunions at my old school take place regularly twice a year for those of us who are able to get there. Sadly, there are fewer of us with each passing year. Of course, for many of us, our childhoods were ruined by the horrors of the Second World War. That is another story, accounts of which can be read in many history books.

Looking back over the past five decades I appreciate that we had many interesting and remarkable experiences as we made our way through the labyrinth of life. As we travelled along it became increasingly clear that you are not one person, but many different people, each with a part to play in place and time. Shakespeare pointed this out in his spot-on poem in As You Like It, The Seven Ages of Man. I wonder if you, our great-great grandchildren, will still be reading Shakespeare at the end of the century? We hope so, but in case you are not I will quote the whole passage in full. Shakespeare wrote it in the 1590s, a different epoch, but the meaning is as true today as it was then. We are now approaching the seventh age of man.

The Seven Ages of Man

"All the World's a stage,
And all the men and women merely players;
They have their exits and their entrances,
And one man in his time plays many parts,
His acts being seven ages. At first, the infant,
Mewling and puking in the nurse's arms.
Then the whining schoolboy, with his satchel
And shining Morning face, creeping like a snail
Unwillingly to school. And then the lover,
Sighing like furnace, with a woeful ballad
Made to his mistress' eyebrow. Then a soldier,
Full of strange oaths and bearded like the pard,
Jealous in honor, sudden and quick in quarrel,
Seeking the bubble reputation
Even in the cannon's mouth. And then the justice,
In fair round belly with good capon lined,
With eyes severe and beard of formal cut,
Full of wise saws and modern instances;
And so he plays his part. The sixth age shifts
Into the lean and slippered pantaloon,
With spectacles on nose and pouch on side;
His youthful hose, well saved, a world too wide
For his shrunk shank, and his big manly voice,
Turning again toward childish trebble, pipes
And whistles in his sound. Last scene of all,
That ends this strange eventful history,
Is second childdishness and mere oblivion,
Sans teeth, sans eyes, sans taste, sans everything."

William Shakespeare

Yet we now have four lovely grandsons who carry in their genes our little claim to immortality. Next year we should have five, since Mary and Larry are expecting a third child. It is for them and their descendants (ours too) that this dissertation was written.

My life really began in 1960, when I escaped from the circumstances into which I was born by fleeing to foreign parts. Only then was I truly independent, and free to do as I pleased.

And what I did pleased me greatly!

Acknowledgements

Thank you, to my husband Jim who shares most of these memories and helped me by adding his comments on the facts as he recalls them.

I am also indebted the helpful comments I found on the web and in Wikipedia, given by others who knew Africa as it used to be.

My grateful thanks go to my editor and publisher Chris Thomas of Milton Contact Ltd. for his vision, enthusiasm and encouragement and for the many hours of hard work he put into preparing the book for publication. His advice and assistance were invaluable.